Inside Out bring̶ ̶ ̶ ̶ ̶ ̶ ̶ ̶ ̶ ̶ ̶ s of familiar
children's stories. ̶ ̶ ̶ ̶ ̶ ̶ ̶ ̶ ̶ ̶ ̶ ̶ ̶ ̶ ̶ the corporate
world needs to get out of their heads and into their hearts,
which will make work rewarding, and profitable at the
same time—Imagine that!

—Linda Ware, author of *Living in Harmony by Natural Law*

Drawing on the power of children's stories, authors Johnson and
Radio have penned their own *Inside Out* versions of several of the
classics like Little Red Riding Hood and the Three Little Pigs. Their
stories will profoundly inform and enlighten you in unexpected
ways. Whether you're in sales, marketing, or management; you will
benefit from the wisdom unleashed in this book.

—Joe Rydholm, Editor, Quirk's Marketing Research Review

I was inspired and a bit surprised that many of the principles in
life are found in the numerous childhood stories that we all
remember. Thank you for following your dream to bring back our
treasured stories and make them relevant to our journey today.
May God bless your efforts and use them to bring change
and challenge to each reader.

—Bob "Bart" Bardwell, Founder, Ironwood Springs Christian
Ranch, and author of *The Marathons of Life*

For thousands of years, children have learned valuable lessons and
insights into the world in which we live through stories. Authors
Johnson and Radio recapture this learning principle by reshaping
classic children's stories for people like you and me. Each is
eloquently retold to enlighten and enrich our soul in
unexpected ways. I've been highly recommending this book
to all my friends and business acquaintances.

—Floyd Roberts, Publisher, Grain & Feed Marketing

INSIDE OUT · INSIDE OUT · INSIDE OUT · INSIDE OUT · INSIDE C
E OUT · INSIDE OUT · INSIDE OUT · INSIDE OUT · INSIDE OU
INSIDE OUT · INSIDE OUT · INSIDE OUT · INSIDE OUT · INSIDE

Rod N. Johnson

Myron J. Radio

E OUT · INSIDE OUT · INSIDE OUT · INSIDE OUT · INSIDE OU
E OUT · INSIDE OUT · INSIDE OUT · INSIDE OUT · INSIDE OU
INSIDE OUT · INSIDE OUT · INSIDE OUT · INSIDE OUT · INSIDE

Beaver's Pond Press, Inc.
Edina, Minnesota

INSIDE OUT INSIDE OUT INSIDE OUT INSIDE OUT INSIDE
SIDE OUT INSIDE OUT INSIDE OUT INSIDE OUT INSIDE
INSIDE OUT INSIDE OUT INSIDE OUT INSIDE OUT INSIDE

INSIDE
OUT

SIDE OUT INSIDE OUT INSIDE OUT INSIDE OUT INSIDE

SIDE OUT INSIDE OUT INSIDE OUT INSIDE OUT INSIDE
INSIDE OUT INSIDE OUT INSIDE OUT INSIDE OUT INSIDE

Using Classic Children's Stories for
Personal and Professional Growth

ISBN 1-931646-93-7

Library of Congress Catalog Number: 2002114932

Book design and typesetting: Mori Studio
Cover design: Kathi Dunn

Printed in the United States of America

First Printing: November 2002

07 06 05 04 03 02   6 5 4 3 2 1

Beaver's Pond Press, Inc.

7104 Ohms Lane, Suite 216
Edina, MN 55439
(952) 829-8818
www.BeaversPondPress.com

To order, visit *MidwestBookHouse.com* or call
1-877-430-0044. Quantity discounts available.

Table of Contents

An honorable mention goes out to our dreams and imaginations. They led us through many narrow and dark corridors from which we emerged triumphantly.

Finally, we'd like to thank all writers of children's stories who provided the foundation and inspiration for this book—some of the authors known, some unknown.

Rod N. Johnson
Myron J. Radio

Celebrate your differences, and downplay your similarities... Your value lies in your differences, not in your sameness... Illuminate your differences for the entire world to see...Your brilliance lies in your differences—your uniqueness—for that is where your seeds of greatness have been planted.

Myron J. Radio

The opportunity is yours to seize... But first you must find the courage to act... To move past your invisible barrier... To move toward your goals, desires, and dreams... And along the way, let your "First Principles" illuminate the way... Only then can you reach greatness, which is your true potential.

Rod N. Johnson

You hold the keys in your hands.
You decide which locks to open.
You decide which doors to leave closed.
You determine which opportunities to seize.
You determine which opportunities to decline.
Remember—You're still holding the keys.

Rod & Myron

Introduction

Our journey to write this book started at 3 am one winter morning. At the time, I was struggling to write a story about the dot-com implosion that occurred in 2000. I awoke, with the nursery rhyme Humpty Dumpty center stage in my mind. I simply couldn't push it away. The next day, I wrote my story incorporating a Humpy Dumpty analogy and sent it to the publisher. Almost immediately, a return e-mail congratulated me on the fresh perspective I took in completing the assignment.

A couple of weeks later, I was reading the Dr. Seuss book, *Green Eggs and Ham* with my son Justin. Justin read the parts of Sam-I-Am, and I read the other character's part. We have read this story more than fifty times, but for some strange and unannounced reason, I picked up a business parallel: how hard it can be for people to change. Wow, I thought to myself. Here I was reading a children's story, and receiving an adult parallel for free.

When Justin went to sleep, I sat back and reflected on the storyline. All I could think was what a truly profound, yet simple story it was.

Every evening when we picked out a different book (although we may have read it many times before), I gained some new insight into the world we live in. Was I the only one picking out these messages? Or could our enlightened scientific and rational minds be preventing us from understanding the concepts that children have always understood?

Shortly thereafter, I decided it was time to enter a domain that I knew little about—book publishing. The youth/adult parallel was so refreshing, I thought. Obviously, there would be a market for a book that told a simple story, yet delivered a profound message. I could imagine walking into the CEO's office of a Fortune 500 company and seeing an array of Dr. Seuss books on the desk. How amusing this thought appeared to be in this complex world in which we live.

But was there sound science for pursuing this youth/adult parallel? Or, was this simply a book that would be entertaining, but of little significance in our personal and professional lives?

I started to research the relevance of the themes and format being explored. My research was full of surprises and encouragement. First, I uncovered that experiences in our youth play an essential role in our lives. These experiences become an integral part of who we are, how we act, and how we face life's many challenges. The unfortunate part: we commonly forget or suppress what we learned in our youth. This insight suggested that my methodology was well suited for those searching for personal significance. Then a second message emerged, one with even greater impact. My search revealed that psychologists commonly encourage people to tap into the healing power and growth energy that lies dormant in their youth experiences. They suggest that by searching our youth experiences, we enable them to reemerge and become a source of illumination. Once again, my goals and methodology were aligned. Lastly, I discovered that the art of storytelling is making a dramatic resurgence around the world. The resurgence is happening in the classroom and in the boardroom. In a world filled with information clutter, stories appear strategically positioned to break through the noise barrier we're all exposed to.

Immediately, I sought out Myron Radio, a business acquaintance I learned to respect. His expertise in the area of organizational development and effectiveness would add another critical dimension to the success of this project, that is, how could we make this real for our readers? Interestingly, he was finishing up his own book, *Dream Makers*, a work that had a similar inspiration. Myron agreed to the concept.

At that point, the collaboration and teamwork was initiated. Before we knew it, the book was coming together, word by word, chapter by chapter. With each passing day, a fresh link to my youth was resurfacing and Myron was tying each chapter to past and present business events. Myron even began to use our stories in public presentations and workshops. As the end approached, our appreciation for life grew more solid. We discovered that we were quickly relearning the value of "First Principles"—the lessons we learned early in life that steered us along a path of adventure, personal growth, and morality. And these lessons appear to be more important than ever in today's complex world.

Inside Out encourages you to revisit the stories of your youth. It provides the perfect vehicle from which you can start to invest in permanent fixes. If you are successful, you will find inspiration, renewed energy, and fresh direction to your life's quest.

Today, as we look across the landscape, it's apparent that many people and corporations have lost an attachment to their guiding principles. It's apparent that we as a society have affixed patches to our souls. When this occurs, the moral compass easily loses alignment, and starts to wobble. Corporations such as Enron, Worldcom, and others yet to be discovered have stumbled. And many will crumble unless they return to the sound business principles told in these stories.

Inside Out is Rod and Myron's journey. A journey that encourages you to change the way you think about the challenges and obstacles before you. To provide balance in a turbulent world. To provide guidance when the stars are misaligned. To be a fresh source of energy and enlightenment to yourself, and those around you.

As you read each chapter, we encourage you to revisit the First Principles you discovered in your youth. We encourage you to make positive changes in your life by breaking down the barriers that prevent personal growth and happiness. We encourage you to use storytelling as a method for better communication with your family, your friends, and your business associates, and as a means of conveying your principles and vision for the future. We're confident the changes you make will benefit you and everyone in your life.

As you go forward, we wish you much success with all you touch and with all who touch you.

Rod N. Johnson
Myron J. Radio

Chapter One

Rod & Myron's Journey

May your dreams come true

Corporate life is always full of unexpected surprises. Emergency meetings to address a flawed assumption in a business plan. A company acquisition changes the alignment of an industry. A lawsuit distracts the management team from their personal and professional goals. An employer announces a significant reduction in the size of their workforce.

This is our story about an adventure in search of meaning, hope, and dreams. It's about being a good friend and how it can unfold into a collaborative partnership. It's a story about how one person's weakness can evolve into strength and enlightenment.

So take a seat and read the letters of discovery that Rod writes as he travels across the country. Then reflect on the daily messages Myron places in his personal learning journal. Whether you're far away or right at home, you too can grow in unexpected ways.

I t is mid-May in the City of Growth. A time when the fragrance of lilac bushes caresses the air of the early morning. A time when spring unfolds into summer. A time when children emerge from the learning halls of school to the playgrounds of their neighborhoods. However, today would change the compass of Rod and Myron's lives forever. For today, Rod would be forced to change his course toward the future.

You see, life for Rod was more than satisfying. It was rewarding at its deepest level. His title was Senior Market Analyst for a major company located in the City of Growth. Rod's position provided mental stimulation, a degree of freedom, and a comfortable lifestyle. It was a great environment to work, to raise a family, and to enjoy life's many pleasures.

Myron likewise had an equally satisfying and rewarding career. He worked as a business consultant, where he built high-powered teams and developed the people within them. Myron traveled throughout the world and loved the variety of assignments he was asked to complete.

Today however, the company where Rod worked would announce a massive layoff. Rod would be one of its many casualties. The corporate public relations department would call it downsizing. The president of the company would refer to it as rightsizing. The numerous employees who received pink slips would simply call it devastating. The remaining employees felt it was demoralizing.

A couple days following the announcement, Rod called up Myron and said, "Myron, this layoff has really affected me. As you know, I really liked my job. To simply hit the streets in search of another job would be hard right now. I guess my mind isn't in the game. Instead, I think I'm going to take a trip. To where, I don't know. I just know I need to sort some things out."

"I understand," replied Myron. "Layoffs are hard on everyone, even those who survive. Where do you think you might go?"

"I'm not sure where I will end up. I think I'm going to start my trip in New York City. It's a city that has suffered through adversity in recent years, yet still maintains its charm and extravagance."

One week later

"Myron, it's time to start my adventure. I wish you could go with me. It would be so much fun to travel together. However, I understand that you must continue to work with your clients. Your job is going to be more stressful than ever. And you must continue to make progress on your book."

"Yes, I wish I could go too. But since I can't make the trip, you must write me and tell me everything you've learned along the way."

"Of course, I'll write," replied Rod. "Anything else?"

"Yes, I do have one last suggestion. Just remember this. The night is always the darkest just before the light of a new day emerges. For some unknown reason, I'm confident that when you come back, something great is going to happen. Good luck and have a safe journey."

"Thank you for your words of encouragement. I will cherish them throughout my journey. And until I return, good bye."

Dear Myron,

I made it to New York safely. What a city! I've been to museums, Broadway shows, art galleries, fine restaurants, and I've met some very nice people. What intrigues me about this city is not the degree of excess that is present on every street corner—rather, it's just the opposite. There is a subtle trend underway toward simplicity. I've experienced it in the museums and art galleries I visited. Great artists like Picasso come to mind. It's present in furniture design and in some of the New York's finest restaurants. I guess one could say Less is More

I'm on my way to Washington, D.C.

Rod

Myron's Learning Journal

The worldwide economy continues to falter, and organizations are beginning to crumble. Some of the world's most profitable corporations are reporting financial inaccuracies and huge losses. It's apparent they moved away from their core values and sound business principles in recent years. Maybe their problems stemmed from an attempt to keep pace with the technology companies. How deep will the losses go? When will they realize that first principles are universal? When will they return to their core values? When will they reinstate their code of corporate ethics?

Companies must focus on getting their corporate structure right. To me, this means governing organizations based on universal business principles that have stood the test of time.

Dear Myron,

I arrived in Washington, D.C. It's amazing how different the monuments look in real life versus what we see on TV. They're really quite elegant and beautiful.

I stopped and visited several libraries along the way. During the summer months, many libraries have children's programs where they have a storyteller present. It's so much fun to watch the interaction between the storyteller and the children. Children seem to learn from the simplest of stories. For example, I saw one storyteller present "The Three Billy Goats Gruff." What an experience! I can only

Dear Myron,

I took a slight detour on my way to see Mickey Mouse. I decided to follow part of the Appalachian Trail south toward Florida. The forests along the Appalachian Mountains are fantastic, yet sad. Here I saw mighty oak and maple trees that stand tall and proud. But in many places, nonnative trees and wild vines were invading these forests. It's beginning to alter the ecosystem of whole mountainsides.

I then started to think about the world in which we live. Here, too, the proud heritage of democracy is being challenged by terrorism. Once proud and strong corporations are being invaded with scandals and lack real leadership. Where does it all end? What went wrong?

Then I started to think about "First Principles," a concept I learned many years ago when I was a child. The lessons that were taught by our parents, our community, and our religious affiliations. It was also taught to us by the children's stories we read over and over again. Has society lost its moral compass?

Wouldn't it be great if we as adults instilled the concepts of First Principles in our lives again?

Rod

Myron's Learning Journal

The organizations I'm working with seem to be getting more strained by the day. Confusion is prevalent throughout the ranks. Employees everywhere are worried about their positions and their livelihoods. Morale has seldom been lower. And now it's really beginning to affect performance.

I see employees everywhere pointing fingers. Their supervisors are adding pressure to increase production and improve quality. Companies need to invest in physical and human assets to get the job done, but I've been told that won't fly. It's hard to keep everyone's head in the game.

Companies need to refocus their efforts on bringing their teams together. Maybe then they can get beyond this bump in the road.

Dear Myron,

I finally made it to Orlando after my brief detour through the Appalachian Mountains. This is such a phenomenal place. A place where everyone can be a child if they want to be.

Back home at City of Growth, I saw too many parents try to relive their childhoods through their children. In some instances, children are put under extreme pressure to achieve greatness. What are these children really learning?

Here in the Magic Kingdom, children can be children, parents can be children, and grandparents can be children. No one seems to care. In many respects, it's expected. It's such a healthy outlet for our busy and complex lives.

Myron, don't you think it would be great if we could implant the youth/adult parallel in today's society?

I'm on my way home. See you sometime next week.

Rod

Myron's Learning Journal

Summer is quickly coming to an end, and I decided to take another time out from work. I literally had to set myself free for a day or two.

I decided to spend the day at an amusement park. Ever since they built the new roller coaster, "The Intimidator," a couple years ago, I've had an urge to go on it. But each time I've chickened out at the last minute. The thought of instant weightlessness followed by a couple barrel rolls was too much.

But I convinced myself on the way to the park that today would be the day. I would conquer my fear of The Intimidator. Although it took me several hours to psyche myself up, I did it. It was as exhilarating as I thought it would be. To have finally pushed myself past my fear factor was quite an accomplishment.

Another thing I noticed today was the diversity of people in the park. Human beings of every race, creed, culture, age, and gender were present. And they were all having a great time. They didn't seem to notice their differences. Instead, they concentrated on enjoying each other and having a good time.

I now realize that our true value lies in our differences, not in our sameness. Our differences "differentiate" us in the marketplace.

Dear Myron,

You may not receive this letter until after I get home, but I had to write it anyway.

Last night I had the most incredible dream. We were in a large auditorium with a stage up front. Every seat was taken; some by parents, some by businesspeople, and some by foreign dignitaries. Guess who was up on stage? You and me! We were just sitting there reading stories from a book. But these weren't ordinary stories. These were children's stories such as "Little Red Riding Hood," "The Three Little Pigs," and "Rudolph the Red-nosed Reindeer." But there was something different. These stories had been adapted somehow to relate to the audience. At the end of our reading, lines of people formed, waiting to meet us and tell us how great our stories were. How they would become a permanent part of their lives. How they would never forget this experience.

Then I woke up, and could not go back to sleep. Never before has a dream been so vivid.

Myron, I know you've studied this stuff before; does it make any sense? I can hardly wait to talk to you about it.

Rod

"Think about it," Myron continued, "the core concepts and format of our book were developed through your letters and my learning journals. Imagine how great it would be if we could teach others about the power of reflection. Picture how many people we could assist, if they understood how this could help them assimilate and integrate all the data they are bombarded with daily. Envision how energized they would then be to achieve their own dreams."

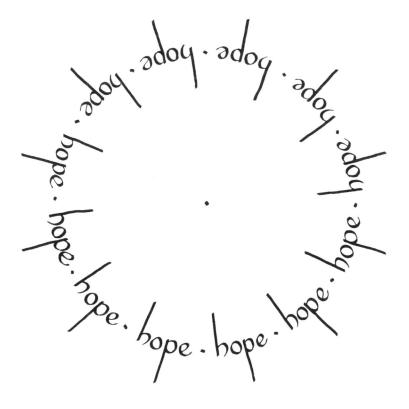

❧ Discovery Notes ❧

The story about Rod and Myron was a journey that encountered hardship, discovery, and opportunity. It was the genesis of their dream. A dream that encompassed a fresh, yet simple book format. A dream that we expect will capture your imagination. A dream that will hopefully inspire you to act.

We found that merely thinking about our dreams and aspirations without capturing them on paper is fruitless. We believe that you must stab these energetic thoughts with a pen and nail them to paper. Then you will be more likely to bring them into your experience.

Rod accomplished this task during his trip by writing letters to Myron. Myron achieved the same end with notes in his daily learning journal. Our reflection on the concepts that surfaced brought us each a calm satisfaction of expectancy that energized us for the journey.

This story is also about the power of storytelling in our personal and professional lives. As you read the story, what emotions did you feel along the journey? sadness? hope? joy? Have you experienced similar emotions to those of Rod or Myron? Have you experienced a dream that you acted upon?

Yes, everyone has a personal story to tell about their beliefs, their traditions, their experiences, their heritage, and their dreams. Yes, every business has a story to tell about its beginning, its value system, its culture, and its goals for the future. Storytelling is the perfect medium to convey your message because it fires up your imagination and then delivers the message with sizzle. It allows your audience to feel what you say in a memorable way.

When you tell a person something, it's like placing pins on a map. You can identify them; it's just that you're unsure of their importance. When you tell the same message in a story, it's like placing pins on a map, and then having the listener connect the pins in the proper sequence of importance for them. The story adds depth, meaning, and importance to your message. It also allows your audience to see themselves in your story. It personalizes the story for them in an inspirational way.

This is why researchers indicate that we are actually wired for stories. Odds Bodkin, a master storyteller states that the spoken language provides a direct link to one's imagination. When this occurs, listeners can identify with images of their own experiences to create an "inner television."

Stories create the connections we all yearn for in our lives that are already filled with information overload. A story delivers the message and then touches the heart and soul of the listener.

We urge you to liberate your creative juices and give life to your daydreams by exploring them further on paper and talking them out with your friends and colleagues. As you do, you will be guided by a higher energy—an energy that will attract your dreams to you.

As you dream, we wish you success and prosperity in material and nonmaterial ways.

Chapter Two
Tilting the Monsters that Lie Within

Poor are those who lose their wit
to question their assumptions
and expectations

The story of "The Three Little Pigs" evolved over the years, with some of the earliest versions dating back to the 1800s. As a child, I can remember playing an active role in the huffing and puffing sequence of the Big, Bad Wolf. The child's version taught us why we must not be lazy, nor take things for granted. If we do, we might perish. Planning, foresight, and hard work are a few of the lessons learned in our quest to overcome the enemy, the Big, Bad Wolf.

Our version of "The Three Little Pigs" holds many of these same lessons—the enemy is our self. How we make assumptions and expectations in our personal and professional lives can be every bit as ravaging as that of the Big, Bad Wolf.

There once was a mother pig who told her three little pigs (Tom, Dick and Harry) that it was about time for them to seek their fortunes. She told each that they would receive $1,000 when they decided the time was right to leave. But they must leave within the next three months. She also warned them that they must each buy a house if they were to keep safe.

Tom, being the largest and the strongest of the three pigs, announced his departure immediately. He had been planning for the day he could leave home, and having $1,000 in his pocket would ensure plenty of good times he thought.

Before Tom left, his mother gave him the money and reminded him of the importance of buying a house. He assured her that he would, and down the path he went.

Before long, Tom came upon a quaint little straw house on the side of the road with a Houses For Sale sign in the front yard. He looked around and thought this would be a nice place to live, so he knocked on the door. A man answered the door and invited Tom in to tour the model house. Upon looking through the house, Tom asked the man, "How much?"

The man replied, "Just $250 if you decide to buy it today."

Tom thought for a second. Wow, this is an awfully nice house for just $250. And that leaves me with $750 left in my pocket to do whatever, like have parties.

Tom turned to the man and said, "Good, I'll take it."

Tom signed the papers, handed the money over to the man, and immediately moved into a new straw house just a few doors down from the model home.

Later that day, Tom painted his name on the mailbox. It read, "TOM PIG."

Not long after this, Mr. Big Bad Wolf was walking down the road when he noticed the new mailbox. Hmmm, he thought, Tom Pig. He would make a nice meal for my wife and family this evening.

So Mr. Wolf walked up and knocked on the door, saying, "Little pig, little pig, let me come in."

"Not by the hair of my chinny chin chin," answered Tom.

"Then I'll huff and I'll puff and I'll blow your house in!" said the wolf. And he huffed and puffed and blew the straw house down.

Mr. Wolf immediately caught Tom Pig and took him home to his wife and family.

Throughout the next week, Mr. Wolf's wife and family would tell him what a great hunter and provider he was. They thought they were lucky to have such a big, bad dad for their father.

It wasn't long before the news reached the newspaper back at the farm where Dick, Harry, and their mother still resided. They found the bad news in the obituary section. It read:

> **PIG, Tom:** age 3, son of Mother Pig, died when the Big, Bad Wolf blew down his house.

Mother Pig and her remaining sons wept for several days. But before long, Dick Pig decided that it was time to seek his fortune.

Mother Pig gave Dick his $1,000 and reminded him of the importance of buying a house.

Dick went down the same path as his brother Tom, and soon came upon the same quaint little straw house on the side of the road. The sign in the front yard read Houses For Sale. He looked around and thought this would be a nice place to live, so he knocked on the door. A man came to answer the door and invited Dick in to tour the house. Upon looking at the house, Dick asked the man, "How much?"

The man replied, "$250 if you move in today." This seemed very reasonable for such a nice house. But then Dick remembered what Tom's obituary said, "died when the Big, Bad Wolf blew down his house." So Dick asked the man one additional question, "Is this house guaranteed against being blown down by the Big, Bad Wolf?"

The man thought for a second, and replied, "No, I'm sorry. This house contains no guarantees against the Big, Bad Wolf."

Dick decided this would not be a safe house to live in and thanked the man for his hospitality.

As Dick walked down the road a little farther, he saw another sign in a yard. This one also read Houses for Sale.

Dick looked at the model house and noticed it was not made from straw, but from wood sticks. Hmmm, he thought. This house looks much stronger than the straw house I just visited, so he walked up to the front step and knocked on the door.

This time a lady came to answer the door. She said, "Good morning, may I help you?"

"Yes, you may," answered Dick. "I saw your sign, and wondered if I could take a tour of this fine looking house."

"Of course. Come right in and I'll show you around," she said.

Upon looking in and around the house, Dick asked the lady, "How much?"

She replied, "$500 if you move in today."

That was quite a bit more than the straw house he had just visited, but this house did look much stronger. Dick decided to ask one additional question, "Is this house guaranteed against being blown down by the Big, Bad Wolf?"

"Oh, let's see. I'm sure there is something in this contract about being blown down by the Big, Bad Wolf," she said. "Ah, here it is. 'This house resists wind damage from the Big, Bad Wolf.'"

Let me see, Dick thought to himself. The straw house contained no clause in the contract against the Big, Bad Wolf. And this one at least states that it resists wind damage from the Big, Bad Wolf (assuming this would be good enough). $500 was more than he wanted to spend, but it would be worth it.

Dick turned to the lady and said, "Great, I'll take it."

Dick signed the papers, handed $500 to the lady, and moved into the new wood stick house just down the street from the model home.

Later that day, Dick painted his name on the mailbox. It read, "**DICK PIG.**"

Not long after this, Mr. Big Bad Wolf was walking down the road when he noticed the new mailbox. Hmmm, he thought. Dick Pig. He would make a nice treat for my wife and family this evening.

So Mr. Wolf walked up and knocked on the door, saying, "Little pig, little pig, let me come in."

"Not by the hair of my chinny chin chin," answered Dick.

"Then I'll huff and I'll puff and I'll blow your house in!" said the wolf. And he huffed and puffed, but nothing happened. He huffed and puffed for a second time, and again, nothing happened. But then he took one last breath, and this time he blew down the house made from wood sticks.

Mr. Wolf immediately caught Dick Pig and took him home to his wife and family.

When Mr. Wolf reached home, his wife and family greeted him, and showered him with accolades. He told them how the wood stick house was harder to blow down than the straw house, but he prevailed. Once again, Mr. Wolf's family thought they were so lucky to have such a big, bad dad for their father. He was such a good provider.

The news of Dick's loss quickly reached the newspaper back at the farm. Harry and his mother found the bad news in the obituary section. It read:

> **PIG, Dick:** age 3, son of Mother Pig, died when the Big, Bad Wolf blew down his house. Proceeded in death by his brother, Tom.

Despite Tom and Dick's passing, Harry knew it was his turn to seek his fortune. Upon his departure, Harry asked his mother for a few words of wisdom.

She said, "Harry, what is the source of your power?"

Harry thought this was a peculiar question and didn't quite know how to respond. So he said, "I don't know."

"You have it!" his mother replied.

"What do you mean, I have it?" replied Harry with a confused look on his face.

"'I don't know'—that is the source of your power. No assumptions. Become part of the forest where you can adapt to all conditions, in all situations. Then you will be truly safe." Upon answering the question, Mother Pig handed her last son Harry his $1,000 and wished him a safe journey and a prosperous life.

Harry went down the same path as his brothers Tom and Dick. Before long, he came upon the quaint little straw house on the side of the road with the For Sale sign in the front yard. He knocked on the door. A man came to answer the door and invited Harry in to tour the house.

Harry said, "First, I must ask you one question. Is this house guaranteed against being blown down by the Big, Bad Wolf?"

The man sheepishly said, "You know what? You're the second pig to ask me that question. And unfortunately, our houses are not guaranteed against the Big, Bad Wolf."

Harry thanked the man for his time and honesty. He continued his journey down the path when he came across the house made of wood sticks with a sign in the front yard. It read Houses for Sale. He knocked on the door. This time a lady came to answer and invited Harry in to tour the house.

Harry said, "First, I must ask you one question. Is this house guaranteed against being blown down by the Big, Bad Wolf?"

The lady proudly stated, "If you look right here in our contract, it states this house resists wind damage from the Big, Bad Wolf."

Harry remembered his mother's last parting words, "Make no assumptions."

So he asked for further clarification. "Excuse me. Resist and guarantee—don't they have different meanings? So I can assume from your contract, there is no guarantee?"

The lady begrudgingly admitted to Harry's point of clarification. There was no guarantee.

Harry thanked the lady for her time and honesty. He once again continued his journey when he came upon another sign. It read House for Sale. But unlike the others, this house was made from brick. He knocked on the door. A man came to answer the door and invited Harry in to tour the house.

Harry said, "First, I must ask you one question. Is this house guaranteed against being blown down by the Big, Bad Wolf?"

The man immediately pointed to a clause prominently displayed in the contract. It stated, "This house is guaranteed against any wind damage and/or from being blown down by the Big, Bad Wolf."

"Thank you," Harry said, and walked in the house for a tour. "How much?"

"$750," the man stated. "Brick homes are the only homes on the market guaranteed to withstand the wind stress of the Big, Bad Wolf. And this is the only one I have for sale."

$750 was more than Harry wanted to spend, but he knew it would be worth it, if he were to be truly safe. Harry paid the man the money, and moved in.

Later that day, Harry painted his name on the mailbox. It read **"Harry Pig."**

Not long after this, Mr. Big Bad Wolf was walking down the road when he noticed that the name on the mailbox had changed. Hmmm, he thought. Harry Pig. He would make a nice meal for my wife and family this evening.

So Mr. Wolf walked up and knocked on the door, saying, "Little pig, little pig, let me come in."

"Not by the hair of my chinny chin chin," answered Harry.

"Then I'll huff and I'll puff and I'll blow your house in!" said the wolf. And he huffed and puffed, but nothing happened. He huffed and puffed for a second time, then a third, and then a fourth. Nothing happened.

Although Harry was extremely nervous at first, his confidence grew each time the Big, Bad Wolf failed in his attempt to blow the house down.

Mr. Wolf was quickly becoming tired, so he knew he had only one last blow left in him. But no matter how hard he tried, he could not blow down the brick house. He walked home that evening to his wife and family who were expecting a nice meal. But there was none.

"What happened?" they asked.

Mr. Wolf went on to tell the stories of Tom Pig who lived in straw house and Dick Pig who lived in the wood stick house, and how he was able to blow these houses down. Then his tone turned solemn when he started to tell about Harry Pig who lived in the brick house. Mr. Wolf didn't understand what happened. After all, he assumed that if a pig lived in a house, he could blow it down. This is what his past had taught him.

Immediately, Mrs. Wolf yelled at her mate. "You dummy! Don't you know you must retest your assumptions on a regular basis? If you had asked me, I could have told you that you would be unable to blow down a brick house. Now I expect you to go back and figure out how to get that pig! Do you hear me?"

"Yes, dear, I hear you loud and clear."

Mr. Wolf could hardly sleep that night, for he had to devise a plan to get Harry Pig out of his house. But worst of all, Mr. Wolf realized that he failed to meet the expectations of his wife and children. He would try not to let it happen again.

The next morning, Mr. Wolf was up bright and early. He went to town and announced himself at Harry Pig's house.

"Dear Pig," he called. "Come with me to Farmer Smith's turnip field. I happen to know that it is full of nice turnips. I will come for you at six o'clock this evening."

"All right," agreed Harry. But he anticipated what was on the wolf's mind, so Harry left the house at 5:00 instead, and gathered all the turnips he could carry. He was back home by six when Mr. Wolf arrived.

The wolf was very angry at discovering he had been tricked, but he did not show it. He said, "It's my fault, I must have accidentally said five when I meant six. Instead, let's meet tomorrow morning at six. I'll meet you here at your house, and I'll show you where some lovely apple trees are at the edge of town. The last time I looked, the branches were heavy with ripe, delicious apples. Great for making an apple pie. If it's okay with you, I'll meet you at six tomorrow morning."

That evening, Mr. Wolf had to go home and tell his family one more time that he was unable to get that pig. His family was very angry. He had failed for the second time in a row. Their great provider was quickly becoming their great disappointment.

But he reassured them he had a plan. Knowing Harry Pig and his bag of tricks, Mr. Wolf reached Pig's house an hour early, at 5:00. He was very angry to discover that he had been tricked once again. But Mr. Wolf decided to go to the apple orchard anyway.

Harry was up in the tree picking apples when he knew something was amiss. He couldn't hear, see, or smell anything. But something had changed, and he knew it could mean danger. So Harry started climbing down the tree, which wasn't nearly as easy as climbing up. About then, Mr. Wolf appeared at the edge of the hill, directly below the tree.

"Good morning, Harry," said Mr. Wolf, licking his chops. "I am pleased to find you here. Tell me, are the apples as delicious as I said?"

"Let me throw you one," answered Harry, and he threw it as far down the hill as he could.

Once again Mr. Wolf's assumptions fooled him. He saw that apple going down the hill, and instinctively thought it was a rabbit, which would have been an easy meal.

When Mr. Wolf realized what had happened, it was too late. Harry had managed to climb down from the tree and trotted home as fast as his little legs would carry him. There he baked himself a plump apple pie to eat.

One more time, Mr. Wolf crawled home with no food for his family. This time, their demands were more explicit than ever. Mrs. Wolf stated, "Our expectations are that you will bring home that pig tomorrow, or else!"

Mr. Wolf knew he was in trouble. But something stuck in the back of his mind. For each time he disappointed, he heard the word "Expectation!" What does it mean, he wondered. So Mr. Wolf stayed up late that night and pulled out the dictionary. Here is what he found.

> **Expectation:** 1) a thing looked forward to 2) an assumption with an ego

Mr. Wolf realized he could never outsmart Harry Pig, so he decided to take a different tactic.

The next morning, Mr. Wolf showed up at the door of Harry Pig with his tail between his legs. He shouted, "Mr. Pig, I need to ask you for some assistance."

Harry paused for a second before giving a cautious reply, "What's that?"

Mr. Wolf proceeded to tell Harry his story and how he could no longer meet the expectations of his wife and family. Did Harry have any suggestions?

Harry thought for a while, noting what a peculiar request this was indeed. But just maybe, there was some hope. After all, his mother's parting words were, "No assumptions." "Am I assuming that Mr. Wolf can't or is unwilling to change? If I were to agree to his request, what expectations would I make up front?" These thoughts and others traveled through Harry's mind.

"Mr. Wolf, I'll accept your request under one condition—we make a commitment to work together, to learn each other's assumptions and expectations. This way, each of us can be assured of a good experience and not be disappointed."

Mr. Wolf nodded his head in agreement.

They sat down and talked throughout the day about their assumptions and expectations.

Mr. Wolf came up with one of the most profound statements that day though. He stated, "Now I see the real problem. Assumptions and expectations are really nothing more than sticks. Sticks that tend to hold us up for a while, but eventually break, and then can be used to push us down. As long as I was meeting my family's assumptions of bringing home the bacon, everything was fine. And each time I succeeded, their expectations became greater and greater. But when this system failed, everything got in the way. Their expectations had exceeded my ability to deliver. Plain and simple."

"You are so right." Then Harry came up with an idea. "You know what, Mr. Wolf? Your family expects you to bring home some food every day. Right?"

Mr. Wolf thought for a second and stated, "Yes, that would be right."

"Well, I know the farmer who owns the farm with the apple trees. You know, where we met yesterday morning. He has a terrible problem with deer eating his apples. You would be perfect for the position of deer chaser. If you agree this would be a good fit, I'll talk to him tomorrow for you. This way you will get paid every day, and with your wages, you can buy food on your way home at the butcher shop."

The rest of the story is history. The Big, Bad Wolf really wasn't so big and bad after all. He was only big and bad because too many assumptions and expectations got in his way. But now Mr. Wolf has the courage to challenge those assumptions. And he has the intellectual power to question the expectations of those around him. Now he can move forward to a higher level of understanding and commitment with his friends, his family, and his community.

And a final note to our readers: As you read our version of "The Three Little Pigs," you may have assumed that you knew how the story would end. Yes, the Big, Bad Wolf would come down the chimney and fall into a pot of boiling hot water—spelling the end of Mr. Wolf. If this was your assumption, we obviously failed to meet your expectations. Accept our apologies if we disappointed you. It seemed appropriate to pursue this alternate ending, since it perfectly illustrates the potentially toxic effects of assumptions and expectations.

✺ Discovery Notes ✺

It's easy to diminish the role assumptions play in our personal and business lives. But they're facing us at every turn in the road. If you have the intuition and wisdom to make good decisions based on sound assumptions, you're able to move forward quickly and strategically. When decisions are made on weak assumptions, the wheels start falling off the cart.

Where do weak assumptions come from? They're generally a product of our undisciplined imagination. We get so caught up in our own story that we lose the courage to remain patient till the truth is known. For example, take a corporate merger or acquisition. When the merger is first announced, employees of the acquiring company tend to be upbeat and expect positive things to happen. Meanwhile, employees of the acquired company experience varying levels of fear, uncertainty, and doubt. Then as information begins to trickle out through the organization of the acquiring company, employees with a positive outlook may begin to express their doubts.

A second example regards the paradigm "the world is flat." Up until the fifteenth century, almost everyone assumed this to be true. This belief was so prevalent, that it deterred the exploration for new territories under the penalty of death. Then one day, Christopher Columbus convinced a group of men to accompany him on a journey into the unknown. At first, the group was excited by the possibilities of proving everyone wrong and returning triumphantly with riches from their discoveries. During their voyage, the expedition experienced strong seas and a devastating storm. Mutiny almost ensued, as the crew was ready to forcefully return to Spain. As they were overtaken by fear, the men assumed they would sail off the end of the earth. Columbus held his ground. And in the end, Columbus would rely on his intrinsic skills, knowledge, and competencies to benefit his crew members and all of humankind.

These examples are similar to our story about the Three Little Pigs. When we don't know the facts, we tend to make assumptions about what to expect. Many times, our assumptions will be wrong. When the true facts are revealed, we take it personally if the outcome is different from our assumptions. We become devastated and feel like we are victims of a personal attack. Why? Because we assumed that everyone else sees the world exactly as we do. We believe others think the way we think, they feel the way we feel, they judge others as we would like to be judged, and they make decisions from a similar perspective.

We know this is not reality, but when these events occur to us, they are "real." Yet somehow, we must overcome our dependence on assumptions. Remember, Harry Pig helped the Big, Bad Wolf overcome his assumption that the only way to feed his family was to use his strength to victimize others. We too must find the courage to remain patient until the truth is known.

Chapter Three
The Leadership Safari

Which path will you choose?

You can temporarily cover over reality with a polished appearance, but reality, in the end, always wins.

Scott Peck

The world needs more leaders. Leaders who can collaborate with the marketplace, rather than conquer it. Leaders who can empower their employees, rather than control them. Leaders who can contribute to the common good, rather than demand it.

But where are they? Are they so focused on proving their success to themselves and their peers that they forget their true purpose in life? Are they so focused on status that their judgment becomes clouded?

These are important questions society must answer. However in the end, one's peers, society, and history will judge each leader. Not by their material goods or social status, but according their value to society as a whole. Yes, maybe success does teach all the wrong lessons.

Yes, leaders must BE complete from the "Inside Out."

Kish, the explorer, and his best friend, Callie Soleil, were walking through the concrete jungle one day, talking about this and about that. As they stared up at the tall buildings, they wondered about who worked in these institutions of commerce. Obviously there were secretaries, accountants, bookkeepers, and salespeople. But who were the leaders of these organizations? Did they have special qualities that made them great? Did they possess magical qualities of presence and power? Were they nice people?

As they pondered these questions, Kish thought that maybe he was a great leader. After all, he was an explorer. And explorers were natural leaders, he reckoned. Famous names like Christopher Columbus, Marco Polo, and Sir Edmund Hillary came to mind.

Callie Soleil, being the mistress of the sun, also thought she must be a great leader. After all, if Kish ran into a problem, he would immediately turn to her for answers.

Despite these quick answers, it didn't answer their original question, "Who led these organizations that are planted in the vast concrete jungle? And more important, what qualities did they and other leaders possess?"

Callie turned to Kish, and said, "I have a suggestion, Kish. Let's go on a leadership safari."

What a great idea, thought Kish. "Yes, a leadership safari. Instead of pursuing wild animals like comatoads and glazzbees, we could pursue leaders of modern society and business."

"But where should we go?" asked Callie.

"I guess if we want to find leaders of the concrete jungle, we should try to think like them. So let's look at road signs, and down streets and alleys as we walk. Maybe we'll find a clue somewhere," mentioned Kish.

As they walked along the road, Callie happened to see a beautiful cat sitting on top of a dumpster in a dark alley. But this wasn't just any ordinary alley cat. Callie was positive this was the Cheshire cat from *Alice in Wonderland*.

They immediately changed direction and walked toward the cat. "Excuse me, Mr. Cat. For some strange reason, I think I should know you," stated Callie.

"Well, that depends on who you believe I am," said the cat.

"Are you the cat from *Alice in Wonderland?* asked Callie.

"Yes, I am."

"Wow, this is quite a pleasure to meet you. Let me introduce you to my best friend, Kish. He's an explorer. And my name is Callie Soleil—Callie, for short."

"My pleasure meeting you," the Cat replied. "How may I help you?"

"We were wondering which way we ought to go from here," said Kish.

"Well, that depends a good deal on where you want to go and what you want to find," said the cat.

"We're on a safari—a leadership safari, that is. We're trying to find the secrets of great leaders," stated Callie.

"Then it doesn't matter which way you go. There are great leaders all around us. Some are famous; some not. Some are rich; some poor. Some are happy; many are sad. Many are good; a few are evil. Some have titles; most do not. Some are driven by money; some are driven by a cause. Some are warm and generous; others are not. Some come from wealth; some from poverty. Only a few will become famous; almost everyone else will not. Some even have buildings and institutions named after them," stated the cat.

"But how do we find them? And where do we look?" asked Kish.

"Oh, if you look hard enough, and walk long enough, you'll find answers to your questions. But beware, leaders come in all shapes and sizes. They are present among all races and religions, and they are all around us. Finding leaders isn't your challenge, my friends. Identifying true leaders from the masses who want you to believe they are great leaders is your challenge," said the cat.

"Let me see if I understand what you're saying. Leaders have no common features or demographic characteristics," said Callie.

"Unfortunately, this is true," said the cat.

"You're also saying that leaders can be found in small and large businesses. They could be rich or poor. They could be white, black, or brown," said Kish.

"Yes, you are correct on all counts, which I'm sure presents great challenges to you Kish," said the cat.

"Why do you say this?" asked Kish.

"Kish, when we first met, you stated that you were on a safari. Most safaris that I know of know exactly what type of animal they are pursuing. This logic will not work in this quest. Your safari is different. Your safari must search at the heart and soul of the person, not their appearance or belongings. In your quest, you will find ordinary people with extraordinary determination. You will find individuals who can instill their convictions and will to those around them. You will find people with a passion that can make it happen. You will notice that leadership is a state of being, not a condition of being," said the cat.

"Then how will we know when we've found a great leader? How will we know we're walking in the right direction, or if we've walked far enough?" wondered Callie.

"Let me say this. You and Kish must learn to listen to your hearts and look through your minds as you search for answers. The success of your safari will not be measured by how far you've traveled nor how high you've climbed. Your success will be measured by how much you have learned along the way. Your safari is just now beginning—and if you're successful, it will never end. If your safari ever comes to an end, it becomes nothing," said the cat.

"Are you telling us that leadership is an unending journey? Are you saying that leadership is as much a science as it is an art form? Are you saying that leaders must have a passion to make it happen?" asked Callie.

"Yes! As you can see, you have quite a journey before you. A journey that will take you to places you have never heard of. To cultures that will seem strange and foreign. To situations that will be humbling, yet very rewarding," said the cat.

"Before we begin the next leg of our journey, could you shed light on one more question that I have?" asked Kish.

"Go ahead," said the cat.

"Where do most leaders fail in their quest to achieve greatness?"

The cat paused for a couple seconds as if to gather his thoughts. "A very good question indeed. Most people who are inspired to become great leaders fail because of human nature. Their intuition tells them they must escape pain and death at all cost, while at the same time they tend to seek out what is pleasant. This basic instinct can be viewed as a state of self-preservation. However, this natural instinct can create unpleasant side effects, and can be directly tied to the moral dilemma many leaders and corporations now face. After all, it's easier to report good news in today's environment. But if you look back through history, some of our greatest leaders resisted this basic intuition. They had opportunities to seek out pleasure, yet they pursued pain and even death in some instances. Great and charismatic leaders like Jesus Christ, Martin Luther King, and Mahatma Gandhi come to mind. Pain may be unpleasant. But leaders must not be afraid of it. They must learn to harness it, for it holds great energy in times of trouble. Does this answer your question?"

"Yes, it does," said Kish.

"Good luck and farewell in your safari," said the cat.

"Thank you so much for your help. And may our paths cross again," said Callie.

Kish just nodded in agreement.

Callie and Kish turned to exit the alley. They had learned so much, yet so little from the wise Cheshire cat. When they walked out of the alley, everything had changed from when they had entered. To the left in front of them was a sign with the name "Easy Street." To the right was another sign, this one with the name, "Success Avenue." And in between the two streets stood a huge park with no name. The panoramic view in front of Callie and Kish was most interesting. Easy Street was embedded with charm and excess. Success Avenue was filled with people in perpetual motion and determined direction. But maybe the park was most interesting of all to Callie and Kish. There were schools of higher education located at the far end of it. In another section, there were large fountains streaming water toward the sky. And in yet another section, there were dead trees, mounds of trash, and homeless people sleeping on benches.

"Callie, do you see what is in front of us? The park is almost like a huge holding pen that people flow into, flow out of, and some seem unable to move—it's like they're caught in quicksand," said Kish.

"How sad—yet at the same time, the park appears very positive and filled with energy. It's apparent to me that people actually have a choice in what they do, where they go, and how they get there!" said Callie.

"Yes, it's a fluid society, isn't it?" said Kish.

"Yes, it is, Kish. Yes it is."

Before they started on their safari, Callie and Kish decided to turn around one last time to see if the Cheshire cat was still in the alley. But to their amazement, the alley and the cat were no longer there. In its place was a long, narrow, and treacherous path that led outward for what seemed like miles and miles. At the beginning of the path stood a sign. It read "PATH to Leadership."

Callie and Kish each looked at the path closely, with awe and amazement. Not only was the path very dangerous, it was obvious that only a few had traveled it. They stood there pondering what had happened since they'd exited the alley just a few minutes earlier. As they looked down the path, Callie and Kish could see a few signs perched along its edge. One sign read "Failure comes easily—Success requires continuous progress and improvement." Another read "Failure is an essential part of our ecosystem."

Without notice, something came over each of them. They began to feel pain, anxiety and euphoria all at once. They started to feel a strong magnetic pull. Yes, they were starting to feel with their heart and their soul.

Callie turned a full 360 degrees, and then turned to Kish and said, "Kish, which path should we pursue?"

Kish, in turn, responded, "Callie, which path do you want to pursue? It's up to you."

✺ Discovery Notes ✺

Leadership goes beyond a charismatic nature. It is more than the ability to excite followers to take a prescribed action, to convince someone to see things your way or to share your vision. While these traits certainly enhance leadership, they are not the sole determinant of organizational success.

True leadership is about optimizing the real assets of the organization: physical, financial, intellectual, collaborative, and human. True leadership identifies with the core value of each individual, and then selects a position that leverages their unique skills, knowledge, and competencies for the sake of the organization as a whole. True leadership builds strong, cohesive teams of people who

1) want to work toward the success of the organization, and

2) feel good about their contribution as they do so.

At the end of the day, a true leader will understand that leadership is a "state of being," rather than a "state of doing," or a "state of having." It's about vision and compassion. It's about morality and self-awareness.

Now go out and lead. You were inherently designed for success.

Now is the time.

This is the place.

You have the power within you.

You have the grace.

You too can make a positive difference in your community, your country, and in the world.

Chapter Four

Breaking
the Shackles
of Fear

*Who we've become versus
who we want to be*

Mark Twain once said, "I have been through some terrible times in my life, some of which actually happened." Such is the power of fear, where we tend to focus on the worst possible outcome to any situation.

The children's story, "The Three Billy Goats Gruff" illustrates this point perfectly. The storyline encourages each of us to challenge our fears in pursuit of greener pastures. If we don't, we are unlikely to realize our true potential. So sit back, and let your emotions and feelings run free in the mountain meadows of "The Three Billy Goats Gruff."

Once upon a time there were three Billy Goats Gruff. The oldest was Big Billy Goat Gruff who wore a collar of thick black braid. Middle Billy Goat Gruff wore a red collar around his neck and Little Billy Goat Gruff wore a yellow collar.

During the winter, the three Billy Goats Gruff lived at the edge of a rocky hillside. Next to their hill was a powerful rushing river. On the other side of the river, a magnificent mountain stood with beautiful meadows scattered about.

If they wanted to graze the mountain meadows on the other side, the three Billy Goats Gruff would have to cross the bridge over the river. But under the bridge lived a great, ugly troll. At least that is what they had been told by their parents when they were younger.

The legend they were told depicted the troll with eyes that were as big as saucers, a head of scruffy brown hair, and a nose that was as long as a broomstick.

"What a terrible creature that troll must be," Little Billy Goat Gruff thought.

"I know that I never want to meet up with that terrible troll. He could eat me up with one bite," thought Middle Billy Goat Gruff.

But for Big Billy Goat Gruff, the thought of the troll was especially scary. For he was terrified of trolls and he was afraid of heights. So crossing a creaky bridge with a resident troll underneath was an impossible feat, he thought.

Every day they would look across the raging river and think how good the grass must taste on the other side. And every night, they would dream about how the fresh flowers might smell. But the images of a creaky bridge with a troll that lived underneath haunted them at the same time.

One evening just as the sun was beginning to set, they decided it was time to find a place to sleep.

So the three Billy Goats Gruff found a nice cozy cave, and entered it. But to their surprise, another billy goat was already nestled in the corner.

"Excuse me, my name is Little Billy Goat Gruff. Would you mind if we share this cave with you for the night?"

"Absolutely not. Feel free to lie down anywhere that fits your fancy. There is enough room for all of us," said the resident billy goat.

"Thank you very much. My name is Middle Billy Goat Gruff."

"My name is Big Billy Goat Gruff. Your hospitality is much appreciated. You know when the sun sets, the air quickly chills here in the valley. By the way, I don't believe I caught your name?"

"Oh, I'm just traveling through these parts on my way to my next assignment. I'm a master Billy Goat. Most just call me Master."

The three Billy Goats Gruff had heard of the Master Billy Goat, but they thought he was only a legend. But he was real. What an honor to share a night with a billy goat of his knowledge and resources, they thought.

"I see you have a nice little valley here," said Master.

"Oh, it's okay. In the springtime, the grass here is lush and ample. But by summer, we have to work hard to find adequate nourishment," said Little Billy Goat Gruff.

The Master Billy Goat thought for a second, "Have you ever thought of grazing up in the mountain meadows during the summer months? My experience has been that the grass and clover in the mountain meadows is so much sweeter and more tender. I think you would truly enjoy it."

"We stare at those mountain meadows every day," said Middle Billy Goat Gruff. "But unfortunately the river is too deep to cross without using the bridge. And we are told there is a terrible troll that lives underneath the bridge that crosses the river."

"And that bridge is very high in the air. For a Billy Goat that is afraid of heights, it just wouldn't be safe for any of us," said Big Billy Goat Gruff.

"Have you ever seen this troll?" asked the Master.

"Oh no, we never get that close to it. But we know it's there," said Little Billy Goat Gruff.

"And, when I was growing up, my parents told me they saw that terrible troll attack my cousin Jimmy Billy Goat Gruff. It was a terrible sight they said. That troll ate him in one gulp," said Middle Billy Goat Gruff.

"Plus, even if that troll didn't live underneath the bridge, which it does, the bridge is too high in the air and creaky for any billy goat to cross over," said Big Billy Goat Gruff.

The Master Billy Goat had heard these types of urban legends before. Their origins varied greatly from valley to valley, but to each billy goat, they were very real and individualized. The symbolic significance of the legends tended to reflect on the shadows of the billy goats' imagination. To overcome the legend, one would have to face its perceived dangers head-on, if one was to emerge on the other side with a renewed soul.

So the Master Billy Goat asked Little Billy Goat Gruff, "What are you really afraid of?"

Little Billy Goat Gruff answered, "I am the youngest. My life's experiences have been relatively easy, and my two brothers have taken excellent care of me. Since I am so young, I'm afraid of the future. What will it look like? Will there be enough grass? Will I find a mate? But most of all, I guess I'm afraid of dying young."

The Master then turned to Middle Billy Goat Gruff and asked him, "What are you most afraid of?"

"I'm most afraid of the present. I wake up in the middle of the night, frightened that we won't find enough food. I'm afraid of losing one of my brothers in a tragic accident. The only way I know how to cope is to live day to day."

"Thank you for your candidness, Middle Billy Goat Gruff. How about you, Big Billy Goat Gruff?" replied the Master.

"I am the oldest and most experienced. I guess I also carry a lot of memories and hardships that I must live with day to day. I guess I'm most afraid of my past."

The Master responded, "It's common to carry fear, anger and pain with us during our journey through life. I want to help you cross over that bridge, so you can enjoy the mountain meadows."

"Did you see that small cedar tree stuck in that tiny rock crevasse when you entered the cave?" asked the Master.

Each of the three Billy Goats Gruff nodded their head yes.

The Master Billy Goat continued, "That tree is several hundred years old, despite the outward appearance of being quite young. You see, that tree's roots are entrapped by the strong granite rock that keeps it in place. Its only nutrients trickle down the side of the rock face, which is very little. Since the tree's roots can't grow deeper or wider, the tree simply grows old—it can never grow up.

"Every time I've visited this cave, it looks the same. It never fosters new growth; it never bears fruit. It simply grows old. What a shame.

"But you know what? As that tree grows older, it ponders how great life would be down the hillside where the soil is rich and ample.

"Do you think it would survive if it were transplanted down the hillside?"

The three Billy Goats Gruff stared intently into the Master's eyes, not knowing what to think.

"I believe it would die there," said the Master. "While its current environment entraps it, the tree has also become dependent on it. Its needs have grown proportional to the amount of nourishment available to it. To put this tree in a new, richer environment would kill it, unless it was properly prepared for the new ecosystem. Dream it may, but I doubt it would survive, unless...unless, it overcame its fears.

"Are you beginning to make the connection?" asked the Master of his class.

Little Billy Goat Gruff said, "I'm sorry Master, I'm still confused. How does a story about a tree help us cross the bridge so we can graze in the mountain meadows?"

"Let's look at your opportunity from a different perspective," stated the Master. "You have probably eaten wild onion roots in this valley."

They nodded their heads in agreement.

"An onion bulb is unique, since it is made up of layers upon layers. The older the onion, the more layers it has. That tree is more than just a tree. That tree is made up of years upon years of experiences and hardships. Each experience, each year is like another layer on an onion. As you peel back each layer, you will eventually get back to its youth as a seedling. A point where its future was perceived to be limitless.

"This process is healthy. Because now the tree can remember what it was like to grow in a land that was abundant. It can heal its wounds at their source, rather than simply growing another layer over its surface. Its reason for living can start from a new and fresh perspective. Now the tree could be transplanted, and grow up, not just older."

"What are you suggesting?" asked Big Billy Goat Gruff.

The Master replied, "I am suggesting this. If you decide to live in this valley till you die, you will only grow old. If you want to grow up, you must cross that bridge, no matter how scary and intimidating it might seem. Let me put it to you this way. The strong Billy Goat does not leave the valley because he hates what is behind him, but because he loves what is in front of him."

"But how?" questioned Little Billy Goat Gruff.

"It will not be easy," responded the Master. "You see, as you grew up, you matured through a process that reflected age and knowledge. As you left your childhood, you entered adolescence. You became a young billy goat, then a middle-aged billy goat, until such time that you eventually die. But as you grow old, nothing really dies. The child is still there; your adolescence is still there. You've wrapped your evolution in layers similar to the layers of that onion. Most of life simply lives on the surface. But to really fix your fears, your anxieties, your pain, you must search back to its source.

As you peel layer after layer back, then you can heal the source, instead of putting one more layer over its ever-present wound.

"The only way to succeed in crossing to the other side is total commitment.

> You must find your youth, if you fear the past.
> You must resist fear itself, if you fear the present.
> You must not fear death, if you are fearful of dying.
> You must not fear love, if what you breathe is the source of life.
> You must challenge your beliefs, if they make you fearful.
> You must become aware, if you hope to find enlightenment.
> You must not fear failure, if you seek success.
> You must not fear what lies over the river, if you love the mountains.

"If you decide to follow your heart, you will find a way to cross that bridge to the other side. No one knows what awaits you as you cross over that threshold. If you decide the risk is too great, then you have decided to only grow old. The decision is yours."

"Then give us some advice. How should we take care of the troll?" asked Middle Billy Goat Gruff.

"It is getting late, and tomorrow is a long day. But I will say this. It will take more than just visualizing it with your mind. You must internalize it in your heart and soul. Then you will find peace with whatever choice you make. And now I bid you good night," said the Master.

When the three Billy Goats Gruff awakened the next morning, the Master had left without notice. It was a bright, beautiful morning as they exited the cave. Each looked at the cedar tree, reflecting on the wisdom bestowed upon them the night before. Indeed, what a powerful story it was.

Several days later, they were grazing in the valley near the base of the mountain.

"The grass sure looks sweet over there!" said Little Billy Goat Gruff. "Let's go over the bridge."

"I bet the flowers smell like honey!" said Middle Billy Goat Gruff. "Yes, let's go over the bridge."

"But what should we to do about the troll?" asked Big Billy Goat Gruff.

They all shook their heads sadly. It was apparent they had not come to grips with their fears quite yet. But that would soon change.

A couple of days later when they were looking at the green mountain meadows, Little Billy Goat Gruff said, "I don't care about that troll. If it's real, so be it. I will not grow old in this valley, no matter how dangerous crossing the bridge might seem!"

Middle Billy Goat Gruff turned to Little Billy Goat Gruff and said, "Count me in. I'm right behind you."

Big Billy Goat Gruff hesitated for several minutes. And somewhat sheepishly he said, "I guess you can count me in. I'll go last."

As they walked in a straight line toward the bridge, a transformation occurred. Little Billy Goat Gruff started to recite out loud,

"My name is Little Billy Goat Gruff and I'm not afraid of the troll that lives under the bridge!" He said it over and over again, louder and louder. Then Middle Billy Goat Gruff followed suit. The noise could be heard throughout the valley.

But Big Billy Goat Gruff was quickly falling off the pace, and was only mumbling the words. It was apparent that he feared the troll the most, despite being physically the strongest.

As Little Billy Goat Gruff reached the approach to the bridge, he turned to Middle Billy Goat Gruff and said, "This is it. I'm going. If that troll comes out and eats me, you'll have the perfect reason to turn back. But I'm going. I'm not afraid of the future and I'm not afraid of dying." And then he started to repeat at the top of his lungs, "My name is Little Billy Goat Gruff, and I'm not afraid of the troll that lives under this bridge!"

Trip-trap, trip-trap, trip-trap, he walked across the bridge without incident. He reached the other side and yelled back to Middle Billy Goat Gruff. "There is nothing to be afraid of. And by the way, the flowers smell oh so sweet over here."

So Middle Billy Goat Gruff approached the bridge and started to yell out loud, "My name is Middle Billy Goat Gruff, and I'm not afraid of the troll that lives under this bridge!"

Before he knew it, he too had reached the other side without incident. The two brothers in turn yelled back to Big Billy Goat Gruff, who was still off in the distance, "It's safe. We both reached the other side safely. We'll meet you when you get here. We're going to eat some of this fresh clover. Take your time!"

Big Billy Goat Gruff was still unsure of himself. He was afraid of the troll, which could be silently waiting for the largest Billy Goat to cross the bridge, he thought. And he was afraid of heights. He just didn't have the same conviction as that of his brothers.

As seconds turned into minutes, and minutes into hours, Big Billy

Inside Out

Goat Gruff realized how vulnerable he would be if he were to remain by himself in the valley. Their strength was as a team, not as individuals. So despite his reservations, he realized he must cross that bridge too.

He approached the bridge, mumbling, "My name is Big Billy Goat Gruff, and I'm not afraid of the troll that lives under this bridge or the height of this squeaky bridge."

What happened next only Big Billy Goat Gruff truly knows. Little and Middle Billy Goats Gruff were grazing in a meadow not far away, but they could no longer see the bridge. Just before sunset, they heard an awful noise coming from the bridge. They could hear Big Billy Goat Gruff pounding his hooves and snorting ferociously. What a tremendous commotion there was.

Little Billy Goat Gruff and Middle Billy Goat Gruff immediately lifted their heads and started running toward the bridge to help. But when they arrived, Big Billy Goat Gruff was just standing there, staring back on the bridge he had just crossed. He was safe, and surprisingly, only a couple of hairs were ruffled.

"What happened? We didn't see it. When we heard the noise, we ran as fast as we could to help," said Middle Billy Goat Gruff.

"Oh, it was nothing," Big Billy Goat Gruff proudly stated. "That dirty old troll started to climb up onto the bridge and I just had to take care of him. I took my two big horns and tossed that troll high into the air, and he fell down into the river below. I don't think we'll have to worry about him anymore."

The three Billy Goats Gruff were happy to be on the other side, where they feasted on the green grass and wild flowers for the remainder of the summer. When the weather began to grow cold again in the autumn, the three Billy Goats Gruff came down from the mountain meadows. And then each summer, they would return to the high meadows once again.

Although they were confident they didn't need to worry, they would cross the bridge saying, "I'm one of the Billy Goats Gruff, and I'm not afraid of the troll that used to live under this bridge!" For it was a reminder of the day when they met their fears head-on, and won. It was also a reminder that fears if left unchecked can grow into monsters, which they vowed would never occur again.

Their world forever changed that one summer day. No longer were their lives restricted to the valley. Just like they had grown to the limitations of the valley, they were learning to grow into the limitlessness of the mountains.

To this day, no one other than Big Billy Goat Gruff knows for sure what happened on that bridge when he decided to tackle his fears. Did that big, ugly troll with eyes as big as saucers really attack him? Or did Big Billy Goat Gruff simply assert his pent-up anger that he had been harboring for so many years against a troll that never was?

We will never know. But then that is what legends are made of.

❧ Discovery Notes ❧

The dilemma that the Three Billy Goats Gruff faced is a wonderful example of how our belief system and undisciplined imagination can hold us back from achieving all we want to achieve, either personally or professionally. Further, it illustrates the sometimes toxic and circular nature of fear. Although the story focuses on the fear of crossing over the bridge, there is a secondary fear present— the fear of staying in the valley. This created a "catch-22," ultimately holding them back from reaching their desires. Some real-life examples could include:

- **Addictive Behavior**—You want to quit smoking. You know it will be very challenging if you are to succeed. After all, you have failed in the past, and you expect you will this time also. If you do succeed, you will likely gain weight, which is a concern.

- **Peer Pressure**—Your friends encourage you to try drugs. You know that drugs are addictive, expensive, and can be very destructive to your life. But if you tell them "no," your social network and environment will likely change.
- **Abusive Relationship**—You're in a physically and mentally abusive relationship. If you stay, you will have financial security and a roof over your head. Plus the family unit will stay intact. If you decide to leave, everything changes; your friends, your home, your financial stability, etc.
- **Life-threatening Illness**—You have an illness that is curable but can also be fatal. If you choose nothing, your life expectancy is three to six months. If you choose surgery, there is a fifty-fifty chance that you will not survive the operation. And even if you do survive, there is only a 30 percent chance of total recovery.
- **Career Change**—The company you work for is constantly announcing staff reductions. You like your job, but you're unsure if or when your name will be announced. If you decide to pursue a career change, you might be forced to relocate, which would be difficult on your family.
- **Changing the Rules**—Your boss demands that you alter some important reports and attach your signature to them. If you follow his demands, you become an accomplice to a crime. If you refuse, you could lose your job.

We all know the feeling. At the moment of truth, we either flee or freeze. Like a rabbit running from its predator or a deer caught in the headlights of an oncoming vehicle, an unknown force overcomes us. This force causes us to procrastinate, make excuses, feel sorry for ourselves, justify all the reasons why not, or pretend that the invisible shackles do not exist. But this behavior will not solve your problem—you need to move forward.

How should you navigate this type of dilemma? To answer this question, visualize yourself as a steam engine locomotive with a dozen railroad cars attached. You've determined you want to change course and pursue a different path. So you head into a roundabout (a huge train switching table used in the 1900s). When you arrive, you meet with the switch master (a mentor, a relative, a friend, a pastor, a psychiatrist, a coach, etc.). The switch master asks where you've been, what goods you're carrying, where you want to go, and whether you have the appropriate paperwork. You're confident the switch master can help you find an appropriate route. Upon asking several questions, the switch master makes a suggestion, which you can accept or refuse. This might mean returning to the track from which you have come, or going on one of many other alternatives.

If you're on the right track; your actions will feel good to you, will be good for you and will serve the greater good.[1] Alternatively, you'll know when you're on the wrong track when you don't feel good about our actions, when you intuitively know your actions are less than right, and when your actions could possibly hurt others beyond yourself. In times like this, a great question to ask yourself is the same one that the Master posed to the three Billy Goats Gruff, "What are you really afraid of?"

> *Fear is conquered by action. When we challenge our fears, we defeat them. When we grapple with our difficulties, they lose their hold upon us. When we dare to face the things which scare us, we open the door to freedom.*[2]

In the end, it's saying, "You won't control me any longer, because I am responsible for me." It's finding the courage to act—to move past the invisible barrier—to move toward the route that helps you achieve your objective(s).

---

[1] Anthony Robins. Date with Destiny Seminar
[2] Wynn Davis. *The Best Success*. (Lombard, IL: Celebrating Excellence, Inc. 1992), 127.

Chapter Five

Executing at the Speed of Thought

Navigating between the known and the unknown

The tale of "Little Red Riding Hood" (originally "Little Red Riding Cap") has evolved over hundreds of years, with numerous variations unfolding over time. Our Inside Out version has added a few new twists and an unfamiliar ending to the story.

As we go through life, we often know where we want to go—we're just unsure how to get there. We refer to this as navigating between the known and the unknown. No matter how diligently we plan for the future, we are constantly subjected to roadblocks and detours. Personal and professional growth occurs mostly by navigating through the unknown. By learning life's lessons well, these obstacles will not hinder our journey; but instead will provide a path toward great accomplishments and personal enrichment.

So lean back, and follow Little Red Riding Hood's trek to Grandma's house. It is full of unexpected surprises.

Once upon a time there was a sweet little maiden. Whoever laid eyes upon her could not help but love her. But her grandmother loved her most. The old woman could never give the child enough. Once she made a present for the girl—a small, red velvet cape. Since the cape was so becoming and the maiden insisted on always wearing it, she was called Little Red Riding Hood.

One day her mother said, "Come, Little Red Riding Hood. Take this piece of cake and bottle of wine to your grandmother. She's sick and weak, and this will strengthen her. Get an early start, before it becomes hot. When you're out in the woods, be nice and good, and don't stray from the path, otherwise you'll fall and break the glass, and your grandmother will get nothing. And when you enter her room, don't forget to say good morning, and don't go peeping in all the corners."

"I'll do just as you say," Little Red Riding Hood promised her mother.

Well, the grandmother lived out in the forest, an hour or so from the village, and as soon as Little Red Riding Hood entered the forest, she encountered the wolf. Little Red Riding Hood had heard stories about the wolf, but she was not afraid of him.

"Good day, Little Red Riding Hood," he said.

"Thank you kindly, wolf."

"Where are you going so early, Little Red Riding Hood?"

"To Grandmother's house."

"What are you carrying under your apron?"

"Cake and wine. My grandmother is sick and weak, and yesterday we baked this so it will help her get well."

"Where does your grandmother live, Little Red Riding Hood?"

"She lives about an hour from here in the forest. Her house is under the three big oak trees. You can tell it by the hazel bushes," said Little Red Riding Hood.

The wolf thought to himself, this tender young thing would be a juicy morsel. She'll taste even better than the old woman. I'll have to be really crafty if I want to catch them both. Then he walked alongside Red, and after a while said, "Little Red Riding Hood, just look at the beautiful flowers that are growing all around you!

Why don't you look around? I believe you haven't even noticed how lovely the birds are singing. You march along as if you were going straight to school, and yet it's so delightful out here in the woods!"

Red looked around and saw how the rays of the sun were dancing through the trees back and forth and how the woods were full of beautiful flowers. So she thought to herself, if I bring Grandmother a bunch of fresh flowers, she'd certainly like that. It's still early, and I'll still arrive on time. So she ran off the path and plunged into the woods to look for flowers. And each time she plucked one, she thought she saw another even prettier flower and ran after it, going deeper and deeper into the forest. But the wolf went straight to Grandma's house.

Time passed quickly. Then a look of utter shock appeared on Red's face. At that moment, Red feared that the sincerity of the wolf was less than genuine. "What if the wolf's intentions were less than honest? What if his intentions were to hurt Granny? What if his intentions were to ultimately hurt me?" Red thought.

Red leaned up against a large oak tree, and deliberated her options. She could throw the cake and wine into the woods and just proceed home, where she would be safe. Her mother would forgive her for not going to Granny's house, due to the present danger of the wolf. Or, she could proceed on her way to Granny's house as planned, with a degree of caution and much fear. The choice was not simple, but it was an easy one. For Red realized that certain choices in life were based on principle, and this was one of them. Red decided to continue on her way to Granny's house as planned.

At that moment, Red began to navigate between the known and the unknown.

Red knew the way to her grandma's house; it was a path she had taken numerous times. Red knew every nook and cranny in her grandma's house; it was a place where she had played countless hours. And she knew that she loved her grandma very much—so much that she knew she had to do something. This, she would soon find, would guide her through a sequence of events that she was not prepared to pursue. But pursue she would, without hesitation.

On the other extreme, Red did not know the wolf's true intentions, or if the wolf had actually traveled to Granny's house. But she had sensed something. Red didn't know how she would defend herself, if she did encounter the wolf. Red didn't know what fears she might encounter, and whether she would find the strength and wisdom to conquer them. But Red knew one thing for sure—a cunning wolf could not be trusted.

Red moved away from the mighty oak tree, and swiftly proceeded back toward the path that would lead to Granny's house. When Red reached it, she looked down at the dusty dirt path to see if there were any signs of the wolf. Sure enough, her intuition was correct, for there were wolf prints leading in the direction of Grandma's house. Red realized there was no turning back; her goal had been set. Her goal was to make sure that her grandma was alive and safe from the potential danger of the wolf. Now it was necessary to create a series of steps that she hoped would lead to a successful completion. Time was of the essence.

As she hurried along the path, she kept thinking about what lie ahead. But suddenly, Red noticed a beautiful rock next to the path. This one was special, something she had never seen before. She picked it up and held it tight in her left hand. It was worn and smooth. But to Red, the rock reflected much more. It was a part of the earth, and she became part of its life force.

Before long, she reached an intersection. Red normally would take the well-worn path to the right, for it was the safest, and was the path most commonly traveled. Although she had never taken it, her mother had told her that the path leading off to the left was a shortcut, but warned that it contained numerous obstacles and hidden dangers.

Little Red Riding Hood clutched the rock firmly as if to find direction and courage. She was not disappointed. She instinctively remembered her goal and her priority for time. She committed to taking the path to the left—the one less traveled.

About ten minutes down the path, Red came upon a stretch where all the trees had been blown down by a terrible storm. What a pity, she thought. But then she remembered one of the many advantages of wearing her red cape—it was a great hiding place for things. She quickly spotted a stick lying on the ground that was compact, yet very solid. She picked it up and thought to herself, "Yes, this will work just fine." She hastily hid it in her cape where no one could see it.

A couple of hundred yards farther up the path, Red came across a babbling brook with no bridge. This was a misstep she had not expected. But there was no turning back; she must find a way to cross it. Red looked upstream and then downstream. There, she spotted a way to traverse the brook. Red quickly walked downstream and leaped from boulder to boulder, reaching the other side safely. Red then realized that rocks from the brook could also assist her in reaching her goal. She quickly gathered up several rocks of various sizes and shapes, and hid them in the pockets of her cape alongside the stick.

It wasn't long before the forest opened into a clearing where Grandma's house was located. Red walked up to the front door where her worst fears were realized. There in the dust were the wolf's footprints.

Red began to pace back and forth in front of Granny's house, just like a wolf would do when stalking its prey. Except in this instance, Red realized she was the prey. Red quickly identified with being a wolf, hunting for its next meal—how it must think, how it must move, how it must surprise.

But then she thought, "A surprise is only a surprise if one doesn't expect it." Red then realized that her success would lie in her differences, her uniqueness, and her preparedness for what lie behind the door. For Red was anticipating the unexpected. And Red knew the wolf would be expecting the expected.

Red stopped for a second, and took a deep breath. She visualized the inside of Granny's house and all the places a wolf might try to hide. She felt inside her cape, making sure the stick and rocks she picked up along the way were secure, yet easy to reach. Red identified with the emotional attachment she had with Grandma, for it would provide her the inner strength and courage she needed.

At that moment, Red realized she was afraid, yet she had no fear. Yes, it was time for the next sequence of events to unfold.

"Knock, knock."

"Who's there?"

"Little Red Riding Hood. I've brought you some cake and wine, Grandma. Open up."

"Just lift the latch," the wolf called in his granny-like voice. "I'm too weak and can't get up from my bed."

Red entered the room cautiously and instantly noticed that the wily wolf was lying in bed, disguised in Granny's nightgown and cap. But rather than pursue the wolf immediately, Red instinctively knew she must play into the wolf's hand, if her surprise were to be successful.

"Come and sit down beside my bed, dearie," wheezed the wolf, "and let us have a little chat." Then the wolf stretched out his large hairy paws and began to unfasten the basket.

"Oh!" said Red Riding Hood, "What great arms you have, Granny!"

"All the better to hug you with," said the wolf.

"And what great rough ears you have, Granny!"

"All the better to hear you with, my little dear."

"And your eyes, Granny; what great yellow eyes you have!"

"All the better to see you with, my pet," grinned the wolf.

"And oh! oh! Granny," cried Red in a sad fright, "What great sharp teeth you have!"

Inside Out

"All the better to eat you with!" growled the wolf, springing up suddenly at Red Riding Hood.

Red had been mentally preparing for this moment. She had already unfastened the stick from her cape and held it firmly in her right hand. Her heart started to pound as she pulled the stick into the open where the wolf could see it. This was her chance, she couldn't screw up now.

Red brought her arm back as if it were a baseball bat, and with all her force, she slammed it across the wolf's mid-section.

The wolf fell to the floor and let out a tremendous howl—one that could be heard throughout the valley. The wolf realized his surprise had not been a surprise at all. He realized that the hunter was now being hunted with a vengeance. The wolf realized that the momentum had turned and it was time for him to exit—and quickly.

Just moments after Red delivered her thunderous blow, the wolf tried to pick himself up from the floor and head toward the door.

Then Red initiated phase two of her plan. She dropped the stick by her side and reached into her pockets, grasping the stones she had gathered by the brook. One by one, Red started throwing rocks toward the wolf as hard as she could.

Before she knew it, the wolf was gone.

Hooray, Red thought. She had conquered her fear, and the big, bad wolf.

"But where is Granny?" Red looked everywhere, but Granny was nowhere to be found.

Red began to cry bitterly, thinking she had come too late. If only she hadn't spent so much time picking flowers. If only she had been more deliberate in her quest to reach Grandma's house. But then, who should walk in but Granny herself, as large as life, and as hearty as ever, with her basket on her arm! For it was another old dame in the village who was not feeling well. Granny had been down to visit and brought along some of her own famous herb-tea.

So everything turned out right in the end, and everyone lived happily every after. But I promise you that Little Red Riding Hood never made friends with a wolf again!

✎ Discovery Notes ✎

Little Red Riding Hood is a wonderful metaphor for the competitive world of business. In our view, the characters and setting represent the following ideas.

- **Red Riding Hood**—The business manager or representative who is seeking to retain a valued customer.
- **Red's grandmother**—The customer.
- **Red's mother**—The business manager or mentor to Red.
- **Red's velvet cape**—The cloak of empowerment.
- **The wolf**—Competition that is seeking to steal your customer or gobble you up.
- **The path**—The business direction.
- **The forest**—The marketplace that is full of competition and distractions.
- **The crossroads**—Choices available to all travelers.
- **Rocks, stones, and sticks**—Bits and pieces of market intelligence discovered along the way that can be used to your advantage.
- **Wolf's footprints**—Market indicators or trends that can only be discovered through inspection.

- **Wolf's arms, ears, eyes, and teeth**—Competitive strengths to be admired but not feared.

In this story, Red strikes out to visit her customer with some gifts of appreciation and to see if she can help them overcome any challenges currently facing their business. Along the way, she encounters a competitor. A funny thing about competitors—when they meet you in the marketplace, they can be very kind and sociable. But you must always realize that they are trying to take business away from you. In fact, if possible, they'd like to either put you out of business or acquire you if it serves them.

Competition is always ready to distract and move you off track. They'll do what they can to change your focus, so they can work around you. They will promote their agenda, while attempting to divert yours. Therefore, when you come to a crossroads, let your guiding principles lead the way. A few guiding principles we utilize in our consulting practices are:

- Short-term gains many times lead to long-term challenges. Stay in the game for the long term and your success rate will improve.

- Stay flexible and balanced in times of uncertainty and stress.

- Focus on your external mission—not on any personal threat.

- Internal motivation combined with external focus is the most powerful way to approach any threat.

- Show confidence and self-esteem in the product or service you represent, and make it clear for all to see. (A Stanford University study showed that physical presence without speaking a word equated to 55 percent of effective communication. The actual words used represented a mere 7 percent, and voice inflection or tonality was 38 percent.)

- Trust that whatever you say will be right for the situation. This will enable you to think quickly on your feet because you are prepared.

Remember—competition benefits the most when your head isn't in the game. Therefore, you must

Stay Focused—Stay the Course—Stay Committed to your Goals!

Chapter six

When Opportunity Knocks— Will You Be Ready?

Finding the hidden talents of your team members

Here's a story about a world-famous leader who was once in jeopardy of disappointing all of his customers in one single night.

This leader planned and executed more than a year for this special event. His sophisticated manufacturing process and intricate supply chain was first class. His product delivery team was composed of the strongest and most powerful performers he could find. Yet on this crucial night, his supply chain was disrupted by a shift in the market environment that grounded this powerful team. Their might alone could not overcome the card that fate dealt them.

Our leader had to scramble. He frantically searched through his organization for someone—anyone—with special and unique characteristics who could step up and lead his team. He found this resource deep within his organization, and the rest is history.

Join us now to learn the story behind the story. It's our edited excerpt from Santa Clause's diary about that fateful foggy night many, many years ago.

I n recent years, now that my beard is getting whiter and my belly bigger (Ho! Ho! Ho!), I've thought often about my friendship with Rudolph.[3] I often ask myself questions such as, "What did I learn?" And as I've discussed some of my emotions with Rudolph, I've concluded it's really a two-sided question. Not only did I ben-

---

[3] Robert L. May, Rudolph the Red-Nosed Reindeer. Lyrics and material to the song by the same title by Johnny Marks.

efit greatly through the experience on that foggy Christmas Eve, but Rudolph did too.

I (Santa Claus) get ready for just two days each year—December 24th and 25th. The other 363 days are spent in preparation. My list includes helping build toys and answering thousands of letters. Then I must select which reindeer will pull my sleigh. And of course, I make sure Mrs. Claus keeps me in shape (after all, I must be ready to eat lots of milk and cookies as I make my deliveries). The expectations of all those children around the world are very high. Timing is everything in my world—known as the North Pole. Thank goodness I have so many workers committed to meeting this demanding schedule. I couldn't do it without them.

But that one foggy Christmas Eve really threw a curve ball into my plan. I had previous experience with fog, but never on Christmas Eve. I simply hadn't planned for such an event. Just like every other year, I had carefully chosen my reindeer for the specific attributes that had made my team successful in the past. For example, Dasher was the biggest. Dancer was the strongest. Prancer and Vixen helped ensure the smoothest landings. Comet was the fastest and Cupid the surest of foot. And Donder and Blitzen were the best at twisting over treetops and skimming over telephone poles.[4] Experience had told me that I had all the bases covered.

But then the weather turned, and suddenly it appeared that my team lacked the basic skills necessary to make a safe and successful journey. Of course, I could have waited a day—but my customers certainly would never stand for it. I had to deliver—my very reputation depended on it.

Suddenly, a reindeer by the name of Rudolph appeared. I had seen Rudolph amongst the other reindeer before, and of course I knew his parents very well, Mr. and Mrs. Donner. And I know that

---

[4] Barbara Shook Hazen. *Rudolph the Red-Nosed Reindeer* as adapted from the story by Robert L. May (1985, Western Publishing Company, Inc.)

Rudolph, like every other reindeer at the North Pole, dreamed of the day he could become one of Santa's reindeer. There was simply no finer honor. For me, Rudolph simply didn't meet my perceived needs of strength and agility.

I never had a problem with Rudolph's red nose, although I knew that many other reindeer teased him and called him names. How wrong I was to think the traits of strength and agility were the only ones important to my yearly schedule. Yes, how naïve I was.

Out of sheer luck and necessity, I blindly came to realize how important Rudolph's red nose was to my mission. And even in years where weather isn't a factor, Rudolph's red nose helps the whole team. We can travel faster, make safer landings, and rarely have to contend with things like treetops and telephone poles. Incrementally speaking, that glowing nose has been the most important asset added to our team.

I give Rudolph a lot of praise too for that day. Here was a reindeer who was born with a glowing nose. Not only was he different, it really proved to be an obstacle for having meaningful relationships with the other reindeer. In many respects, he was an outcast with very few friends. Yet regardless of the circumstances, Rudolph was always there ready to help anyway he could. He so desperately wanted to become part of the team.

I'm sure he kept asking himself, "Why can't I be just like the other reindeer? Why can't I have a small brown nose, instead of a big, bright, red one?" When you're young like Rudolph was, I'm sure he searched for answers when there were none.

Inside Out

But some how, Rudolph found the inner strength that kept him focused from day to day. And when I needed help, Rudolph was there ready to assist, anyway he could. I guess I could say, "When opportunity knocked—Rudolph was ready." Not only did his red nose help me navigate through the difficult fog, Rudolph also exceeded my every expectation. His leadership skills were excellent. His navigation skills were second to none. His ability to quickly rebuild and refocus the team of Dasher, Dancer, Prancer, Vixen, Comet, Cupid, Donder, and Blitzen was remarkable. All along, I had this tremendous asset directly under my nose and I never realized it.

In retrospect, this incident made me a much wiser man. It taught me that looks and sheer strength aren't everything. It taught me that I must look outside my comfort zone to find the hidden value amongst my team members. It taught me that I can never be too prepared. Yes, I must plan for the unthinkable. It taught me that even nonconformity can be an asset to an organization.

It also revealed an inner strength that I possessed. Somehow, some-way, Santa Claus was going to deliver according to plan—on time! My reputation was on the line. The days and months of hard work amongst all my team members was at stake. If I didn't deliver, I would have failed myself, I would have failed Mrs. Claus, I would have failed my team members, and most important, I would have failed thousands of girls and boys. No excuse was acceptable!

Yes, that Christmas Eve taught me a lot. Yes, that Christmas Eve taught Rudolph and all the other reindeer a lot.

Today as I write in this diary, I think about how much has changed in recent years. It's simply mind-boggling. In years past, all the boys and girls of the world would sit down at the kitchen table, write me a letter, and then place it in the mail. Today, so many children write to me at the North Pole via e-mail, it seems peculiar not to have stacks of mail sitting at the North Pole post office. But that one magic Christmas Eve, I learned the most important lesson of all. I must adapt and consistently prepare to meet the needs of my customers, the boys and girls of the world. Whether it is one day a year or 365 days a year, my commitment would be the same. And I will do everything in my power not to disappointment.

Good night, Mrs. Claus. Good night Dasher, Dancer, Prancer, Vixen, Comet, Cupid, Donder, and Blitzen. Good night to all the elves and helpers that make Christmas possible. Good night, boys and girls of the world. Good night, diary. And good night to the most important reindeer of them all—yes, good night, Rudolph.

Santa Claus

❧ Discovery Notes ❧

Upon first reading the story of Rudolph, one might surmise that it is a nice story, but somewhat unrealistic. Yet the story is a powerful metaphor for valuing differences in the workplace and in life.

Think for a moment about how unrealistic the following headlines are:

- A 34-year-old copywriter for the Montgomery Ward company is given the assignment to develop a Christmas giveaway booklet. The story, "Rudolph the Red-Nosed Reindeer" is now immortalized in print, song, and television—**Robert L. May.**

- Two sisters from the inner city dominate the tennis world—**Venus and Serina Williams.**

- A tall, lanky high school grad becomes a trusted coach and advisor to heads of state and sports champions around the world—**Anthony Robbins.**

- A senior citizen embarks on a cross-country mission to sell his chicken recipe to private restaurant owners—**Colonel Sanders.**

- Two bicycle storeowners from the American farm belt decide they want to fly. In the process, they spawn a new industry—**The Wright Brothers.**

- A 3-year-old African/Asian/American child hits golf balls on late night television and goes on to dominate the sport—**Tiger Woods.**

- A woman breaks through the perceived "glass ceiling" to become the CEO of Hewlett Packard/Compact—**Carly Fiorina.**

- An overly enthusiastic, chain-smoking, clown-suit-wearing, peanut-chucking executive leads Southwest Airlines to consistently positive financial results even when other industry giants are losing millions—**Herb Kellerher.**

- A young nun, frustrated at not being able to gain medical attention for a dying man forms the Missionaries of Charity, in Calcutta, India—**born Agnes Gonxha Bojaxhiu, she became Mother Theresa.**

- A man "without letters" (no formal education) is recognized as the world's greatest genius—**Leonard De Vinci.**

- A wild-eyed, braggadocio young boxer whose license was revoked for following his religious beliefs lights the torch for the 2000 Summer Olympics and brings tears to the eyes of millions around the world—**Mohammed Ali.**

- A world-class athlete is diagnosed with testicular cancer. At one point during his treatment, he is told he has a 2 percent chance to survive. He beats the unbelievable odds, and then proceeds to become one of the most dominant bicycle racers ever in the Tour de France—**Lance Armstrong.**

- A college dropout and computer geek with a violent temper becomes one of the world's richest people and greatest philanthropic contributors—**Bill Gates.**

This list could go on and on. The stories are the same. Genius and determination were buried within the human frame. They overcame daunting odds to achieve greatness. And none of their greatness would be possible unless someone along the way recognized it and then encouraged them in their quest.

So how does this happen in organizations today? How are unassuming or different people identified? How are the seeds of greatness within nourished and cultivated for success?

According to a Gallop study,[5] one of the most effective approaches managers can use to enhance the performance of their organization is to fully utilize each person within the organization based on the individual's unique set of skills, knowledge, and competencies relative to the job at hand. This means

- selecting the right people for the right job,
- setting the desired outcomes and/or expectations,
- motivating and/or coaching them on their strengths, and
- promoting them into the next right job based on these same criteria.

Remember, your value lies in your differences, not in your sameness. When you accentuate your differences, your performance and the performance of your entire team will be noticed. In the process, you just might change the world.

---

[5] Adapted from First, *Break All the Rules* by Marcus Buckingham and Curt Coffman.

Chapter Seven

Consistent-Is-My-Name, Persistent-I'll-Be, Change—Not Me!

Is this your opportunity to grow?

"Change" has been with us since the beginning of time. In fact it's been said that along with dying and paying taxes, change is the only other thing we can absolutely count on. Change is our pathway to growth, for growth cannot occur without change. Yet most people we know are adverse to change. It can strike fear in the hearts of the brave and even worse in the minds of the weak.

The following story brings to light how difficult it can be to change in a corporate setting where consistency is valued and rewarded. But over time, the need to change becomes a critical success factor for all organizations. How a leader encourages and facilitates the change process with their individual employees is crucial to the business unit's success.

The essence of change is important to everyone. As you read our story, think of how you and others you know might react in a similar situation.

Consistent has been my name since birth!
And Persistent-I'll-Be has been my trademark here on Earth.
For these elements are an important part of me, you'll soon see.
Because that's how everyone has come to know me.

My boss tells me I'm the best!
Never worry says he in jest,
your job is safe, not necessarily all of the rest

Consistent you are, says he
and equally persistent you tend to be.
These ideal traits do please me.

Then one day my boss came up to me.
He said, "Consistent, do you like change?"

"No, no, no," said me.
"Change—not me!"

"Don't you remember, my name is Consistent,
and don't forget, Persistent-I'll-Be,
but to change—don't ask me—please."

But my boss, also being a persistent kind of guy,
had a vision in his eye.
He thought change would be good,
so he said, "Would you please change—just for me?"

"I will not change,
not for you, not for me.
Just let me be,
just let me be the person you encouraged me to be!"

"But you must change," said my boss to me.
"You see, I also have a new boss who manages me.
He tells me, out with some of the old and in with some new.
This is our quest at Old Way/New Way," according to he.

"But wait, not so fast and furious," said I.
"Consistency is good in our customer's eye,
and persistency is required if we are to succeed,
but now you're asking me to change so many things—I don't
  necessarily agree!"

"I'm not saying it will be easy," said my boss to me.
"Not for you—not for me.
I'm just asking you to learn some of the new,
while at the same time, unlearn some of the old—do you see?"

"I'm sorry," I said.
"I want to enjoy each day as it comes,
and let it come as it may.
But please don't ask me to learn a new and different way."

"Performance is the reason we must change," said my boss.
"What was perfectly OK yesterday is tomorrow's loss.
Now I know old habits die hard," he reassured me.
"But I can assure you, this is important for you and for me."

My boss went on to say, "You don't like change—so you say.
But try it once, try it twice, and you may.
Try these changes and you may."

In response to his voice of plea, I said,
"If I try it once,
if I try it twice,
and I don't like it,
will you then just leave me alone—please?"

"I wish I could say yes to your simple plea,
but sooner or later, we must all change, don't you agree?" said my
    boss to me.
"Sooner or later, you'll understand the need,
the need for change is as important to you as it is to me."

"If I say yes to your plea,
will you be there for me during my times of need?
Will you be there when I'm just tired, frustrated, or peeved?
I need to know this if you want me to unlearn the old while I learn
    the new."

"Consistent, I'll make this promise to you.
I'll be there to help you along the way, you'll see.
I'll give you feedback during times of need,
and, I'll give you praise when you succeed.

"I know that change is not easy,
not easy for you,
not easy for me.
But change is good, you'll see—just trust me.

"The CEO says new is good,
and to achieve our goals, we must change.
Everyone at Old Way/New Way will change,
you'll see."

"Okay," I said hesitantly.
"Today is the day.
Yes, I'll agree to your persistent plea.
I just hope my consistency and persistency will lead me to
tomorrow's success."

"I know you can do it," said my boss with much glee.
"I know you can do it," he said confidently.

6-Months Later

Consistent has been my name since birth,
and Persistent-I'll-Be has been my trademark here on Earth.
Change—I thought I would never do,
but now it's fun, cause I know exactly what to do.

Ten years of "in the know" was part of the old.
Six months of constant change is the part of the new.
Old is not bad—at least not according to me.
It's just that the new way is so much more challenging to our team.

We must think fast on our feet,
since we must handle all kinds of situations we'll inevitably meet.
But we can handle the stress,
no matter how difficult the test.

There are risks we must constantly face,
but we see these as opportunities—not obstacles that hinder our
    pace.
Success is our goal that moves us toward great ways.
Success is our goal at the Old Way/New Way today.

❧ Discovery Notes ❧

Change is a facet of life that is accepted or rejected in a variety of
ways. Some people readily adapt to change and often thrive on it.
Others may not even recognize that things are changing around
them until it is specifically pointed out to them. Still others accept
change only if they are warned in advance that it is coming—and
then reluctantly. And finally, there are those who will hold on to
the status quo as long as possible.

Our experience has shown that one's personal acceptance or rejec-
tion of change is tied directly to one's ability to deal with uncertainty in their life and still feel a sense of control. The question
everyone must answer, Do you want to lead the inevitable changes
that you will face in the future (cause), or are you willing to be
swept up by them (crisis)?

There are three distinct types of change that you might encounter.
The first type is *Evolutionary* change. Evolutionary change is initiated to gain incremental improvements in programs, processes, or
structures. Examples include

- Efforts to keep up with the competition.
- Minor tweaks in an organizational structure.

- The introduction of new products and/or services.
- Personal performance improvements achieved through attending a workshop or training session, etc.

The second type, *Revolutionary* change, reaches the next order of magnitude and is progressively more difficult to accept by the masses. It includes changes that must be made by organizations if they are to survive in the marketplace. Examples include

- A change in a market forecast precipitated by altered supply.
- Lost market share.
- Demographic shifts.
- A cash flow reduction.
- Right-sizing initiatives.
- Outsourcing initiatives, etc.

Finally, there is *Chaotic* change. This is the type of change that no one can predict. Examples include

- The stock market crashes.
- An acquisition or takeover by a competitor.
- A terrorist attack.
- Major defalcations.
- Accounting misrepresentations or errors.
- Overnight product obsolescence, etc.

Regardless of the type of change you may encounter, it is important as a leader to always help your associates navigate through their personal change curve. Our rendition of the change cycle has been adapted from the work of William Bridges.[6] As we see it, this cycle has four distinct phases.

1   **Stage 1—The Ending:** This stage signifies that an area of our life is about to end—for good or bad, depending on

---

[6] William Bridges. *Managing Transitions: making the Most of Change.* (perseus Publishing, 2nd Edition, December 1980)

one's personal view. It means that we are about to under-take a change that either we ourselves initiated in hope of improving our position in life, or one that was thrust upon us by an outside force (another person, the organization, the economy, etc.). The positive aspects of this stage are characterized by optimism, excitement, anticipation, bold-ness, and enthusiasm. The negative aspects are represented by worry, anger, belligerence and shock.

2   **Stage 2—The Valley of FFUD:** FFUD is our acronym for fear, fatigue, uncertainty, and doubt. These characteristics can make cowards of us all. They can invoke distraction, defeatism, desperation, victimization, and a sense of being stuck in a place with no way out. Overcoming the mental and emotional obstacles in Stage 2 is critical to our success. We do this by using our critical thinking skills and taking one step forward at a time.

3   **Stage 3—The Moment of Truth:** Once we move through Stage 2, we begin to experience some of the results we are searching for. If we accept these results in a positive fash-ion, we can transition ourselves to Stage 4. If we view the results as a one-time occurrence or don't deem ourselves worthy enough to move on, we will slip back into Stage 2.

4   **Stage 4—The New Beginning:** This final stage is charac-terized by transformation, a sense of accomplishment, gratitude, and increasing hope for future success. In organ-izations, "The New Beginning" simply becomes the way we do business.

Evolutionary change will closely follow this four-stage curve. However, when people are exposed to revolutionary and chaotic change, they may move instantly into Stage 2. If this occurs, it is the leader's responsibility to provide certainty and steely calm to the situation. This will enable your associates to move through the change cycle successfully and with less stress.

Implementing a major change requires one to adjust their thinking pattern or mindset. When we change the way we think about a given problem, a change in our behavior and/or action will occur. Recognizing and rewarding behaviors (either positive or negative) in an organization will help drive performance toward the objective.

Once a change has been implemented, the optimum means to sustain the momentum is to

1) Measure your results and publish your findings, and
2) Reinforce positive behaviors whenever and wherever you encounter them.

It is important to stress that leaders should be prepared to assist their organization through various change cycles. When the fear of change can be reduced, objectives will be achieved sooner and more completely.

Chapter Eight
How Me was Changed to We

The power of teamwork
cannot be overrated

Teams, teams, teams. We see teams everywhere we look. Teams are espoused as the keystone of organizational values. Yet as we take a deeper look at actual operation, what organizations need less of are teams. Instead, what they really need is more teamwork.

For an employee to be a team player, they must first understand the value they add to their team. The team must acknowledge this unique value, and then accept each individual as an important resource to the team's overall success. The process all starts with the team leader. But too often, leadership is about personal significance rather than team performance. We hope that our story will teach a priceless leadership lesson.

E very employee in Workerville came to work a lot. Some four, some five, some six days—it really was a lot.

Now, it wasn't the work that the employees deplored. Quite to the contrary, it was the work they adored and more. They met many friends at work—it meant a lot. They knew how to sing Happy Birthday when that special day came about. They'd gladly share gifts during festive occasions. And yes, they would all stand tall and close together during times of sadness and joy. Their friendships meant so much more than their work and their Workerville chores.

The employees at Workerville would start their day right every morning. They would say to their fellow workers, "How are you this fine morning, my friend?" And they would respond, "Fantastic, and a good morning to you galore."

But amongst the workers in Workerville, there was a worker that just didn't seem to fit. It's not that he was different, not one little bit. But rather, he looked quite ordinary, as strange as that may seem. It was his manners they deplored, not he.

All the workers would pretend to be his friend, but they were not. The workers would share their joys and sorrows, but he would not.

His name was Jack. A simple name indeed. But to most of the employees in Workerville, his name was Boss. Mr. Boss to you and me.

Jack would start the day early, in by seven or before. There was never a minute to waste, nor a day off to be bored. Time was just too short, according to his calendar, which he adored.

TO WASTE IS TO LOSE
AND TO LOSE IS TO WASTE

was the sign that hung on his door.

Now Jack was a wondering and pondering kind of guy. Every spare minute was spent wondering about this and pondering that. His wondering and pondering was usually about all the employees in his Workerville plant. "Now let me see, how I could squeeze this and how could I squeeze that," thought he. It was all about squeezing just one more ounce of work from every employee who works for he.

Every once in a while you'd hear from behind his door with much glee, "Aha, yes, I have found just one more squeeze!"

Now the employees down in Workerville didn't like the man they called Mr. Boss one bit. Except for just one—who seemed to like him just a little bit.

His name was Junior McGlee, an unusual name indeed. And yes, he liked all the usual things, just like you and me.

Now Junior McGlee was like every other employee, in by seven and out by three. For some strange reason of which no one could make sense, Junior McGlee saw good, not evil, in the man they chose to resent.

No matter how hard and shrewd Mr. Boss would be, the squeeze never so much as created a wheeze from Junior McGlee. The squeeze was expected by Junior McGlee, although he thought it was very strange indeed. Junior McGlee would simply ask, "Why Mr. Boss, do you work so hard just to squeeze, squeeze, squeeze?"

But Jack was very smart indeed. "Why, Junior," he would say, "it's all about achieving this and achieving that. It's about me and it's about that."

But Jack mentioned a this and a that one too many times. "Uh-oh," shouted Junior McGlee, as he raised his ear toward the ceiling as if to see. "Did you hear a that and a this—it doesn't sound too good to thee."

Now Jack being the nervous boss he be, immediately perched his ear in the air to hear what Junior McGlee thought he could see. But all he could hear was the sweet humming of so many worker bees. "It sounds just fine to me," said he. "I don't hear anything different, not according to me. Yes, everything sounds just fine to me, McGlee."

"Oh, but no that is not the case. If you listen carefully, you'll hear a squeeze too many here and a squeeze too many there," said Junior McGlee.

Now Jack, who thought you could never find too many a squeeze, found this message a little strange indeed. "What do you mean? I don't understand," said he. "Don't you know, a squeeze is a squeeze, where there is no such thing as too many when I'm talking about my worker bees."

But then a strange thing came over Jack, for just one moment it seemed. The boss suddenly heard squeaks, a strange noise for he indeed. "What did it mean? What did it mean?" he shouted in vain. A squeak is not good, and especially not two or three.

But the squeaks in his brain grew louder and louder to his demise. Could Junior McGlee be possibly right? Could the hum of a squeeze really have been a squeak in disguise? "Oh, what a problem indeed," said Jack as he turned to Junior McGlee.

Now Junior McGlee, the sound thinker he be, told Jack "Oh, don't worry, I believe in thee. You see, I think you have learned an important lesson today. It's not about 'me', it's all about 'we,'" said McGlee.

For Jack, the word "we" was a foreign concept at that. So he asked, "You mean 'we' is more important than 'me' when running the Workerville plant?"

"Oh, yes, you'll see in due time," replied McGlee. "The vision of 'me' is like a fish with no sea. The embrace of 'we' will make you strong in the eyes of the Workerville bees and me."

About that time, Mr. Boss suddenly became Jack to most. And every employee at the Workerville plant came up to Jack to say, "How are you this fine morning, my friend?" And to Jack's amazement he would shake their hand and say, "Fantastic, and a good morning to you and more."

Then Jack pondered for a minute or two. How could this be so, he thought to himself. Could it be that the term "me" was really all about "we," as he moved across the work floor.

Then Junior McGlee shouted to Jack with glee, "Do you hear that?"

Jack raised his ear as if to see. "Yes, I do hear that," he delightfully shouted to Junior McGlee. The squeaks had been replaced with hums, where squeezes once were placed. One by one, the sounds that were all about this and that, became sounds of "we" at the Workerville plant.

No sweeter sound could ever be heard. After all, from that day forward, the word "me" was never heard from again.

❧ Discovery Notes ❧

Organizations throughout the world have stated objectives that indicate something similar to one or more of the following:

- Achieve "Best In Class" status within our industry.
- Become the lowest cost provider of goods and services within our market.
- Drive costs out of our business.
- Meet or exceed our customer's expectations.
- Value and/or empower our employees.

In effect, these organizations are really saying they want their operations to hum, to delight their customers, to keep their employees happy, and to give major stakeholders (stockholders, private investors, or venture capitalists) a feeling of certainty about their investment. Yet how many companies actually achieve and sustain these results? Not many. Why? It's because their actions are not consistent with their words. Essentially, they neither "walk their talk," nor do they change the way they recognize, reward, and compensate their organization for the new behaviors that are required to achieve such lofty goals.

As an example, a company we know stated they wanted to provide world-class customer service as a means of building market share and bottom-line profits. In the past, star performers were recognized and rewarded with promotions and growth assignments regardless of their team skills. The company's leaders realized that to effectively provide world-class service, they would need to change their culture or their rules of the road. The new culture would have to value team performance over individual performance. Despite their new strategic intent, the leaders continued to reward star performers over team performers, without cognitively comprehending what they were doing. As a result, their customer service initiative soon lost its luster, and the leaders began to search for another program to positively impact the bottom line.

Another organization undertook a similar initiative and culture change, but this one proved to be successful. Like the first organization, this company completely changed the way they conducted their business operations. Work processes were reengineered to emphasize customer focus. Entire departments were reorganized, restructured, and restaffed with employees who had demonstrated customer and teamwork competencies. Even the focal point of management's oral and written communications changed to emphasize the importance of teamwork in delivering world-class customer service.

Yet all of these positive efforts still weren't enough to successfully shift the organization's culture. The actual shift effectively occurred the day a notorious and abusive star performer was removed from the job and replaced with a well-recognized team leader. With this single bold leadership stroke, the rules of the game changed forever. Almost overnight, the organization began to enjoy team success. As customer feedback grew more positive, the company began to draw business away from the market leader at the time. Then the word spread across the industry that a new player was on the block; a player who had reinvented itself; a player that meant business. It wasn't long before the competition started to kick off customer service campaigns, but none could match the success of this new market leader.

How long can newly invented teamwork and a customer-service culture endure? It will thrive as long as the leader at the top of the company supports and actively promotes these values. Why? Because people in organizations want and need leadership—they want and need someone to "lead their ship." Initially, the corporate ship will maintain its course even when a new leader with a different set of values arrives on the scene. However, any change in perceived and stated values will ultimately steer the organization in a different direction if it comes from the person leading the ship. Herein lies the dilemma of changing leadership. It's not only initiating the change that takes concentration, clarity, and focus. It also takes constant vigilance, intelligence, and attention to sustain the change momentum. In effect, it's a combination of leadership and personal rewards and/or consequences that makes the difference over time.

Chapter Nine
The Moral
Dilemmas
We Face

*Will your values and code of
ethics withstand the pressure?*

The flood of stories about immorality within the business community and by its leaders is disturbing. What happened to the moral codes of conduct and principles that were supposed to guide us through difficult times? Did they disappear? Did they become unfashionable? Did they lose favor in today's results-driven society? Our story reflects on the moral dilemmas we must ultimately face.

John Locke sets the stage. He noted, "We are a kind of chameleon, taking our hue—the hue of our moral character—from those who are about us."

The question is, Are you ready to step up and make the righteous decision? Or will you succumb to the expectations of your environment and peer group? So sit back and place yourself in the challenging world of corporate expectations.

O nce upon a time,
not so long ago,
there was a company dominated by a prominent CEO.

His name was Bernie,
a shrewd player was he.
A shrewd player that was always looking for opportunities.

The press admired him, as he spoke eloquently of corporate greed.
His investors loved him, as he delivered them consistent proceeds.
And Wall Street cherished him, as they showered him with attractive IPO's.

But his friends all knew, it was just too good to be true.

They all knew his talk of good fortune would eventually come unglued.

But that did not slow Bernie in the least.

He just kept talking about the size of his corporate piece.

Options were the enumeration he adored.

Options were the compensation his Board liked to explore.

The annual stockholder's meeting was a day Bernie looked forward to.

Because the press, Wall Street, and his peers would listen to every word he'd put forth.

And to no one's surprise, Bernie bragged about the growing size of the corporate pie.

The unsettling part of course, it was just a big lie.

The next day, Bernie's picture was there on Page One of the financial news.

The newspaper gave him high praise for his prowess and futuristic views.

It noted that Bernie could spin glass into gold,[7] a comparison to a modern day Rumpelstiltskin.

Meanwhile at Corporate Headquarters

Only a few had shown up for work on that peculiar Saturday.

With each of us working on our own special tasks.

Wendy and I were calculating the size of the corporate pie that reflected our past.

---

[7] Spinning glass into Gold refers to the use of fiber optics in data and voice communications.

We knew as we crunched the numbers we two.
It was not going to look good to the bosses we reported to.
Expenses too high, margins too low.
Sales too slow, yes, sales were too slow.
All of these things we would have to show.

We sat there pushing numbers we two.
When suddenly the door flew open to our surprise.
We heard a thump,
a thump that startled us from our focus on our imminent earnings
   slump.

We looked toward the door to see what had happened.
And there we saw a man,
a little man with a bright red feather pinned to his Robin Hood cap.

In he walked, directly into our room.
Then he said to us, "Good afternoon, you two.
Why do you sit there with such gloom?
I know it is cold and damp outside.

And I can tell from your faces, you're holding onto an unpleasant
   surprise.
But is it really worth it, in the big scheme of things?
Is it really worth, contemplating so many unpleasant happenings?"

So we asked him, "Excuse me, do we know you?"

"Well yes, I think you do.
Have you ever heard of a man who could spin straw into gold?"

We thought there for a second we two.
Could it be?
Could it be so?
Could it be Rumpelstiltskin?

We asked if it could be so.
And to our amazement, he stated it was true.
We then proceeded to tell him about our impossible task.

"I have a great idea to help start the day anew," he professed with
   great confidence.
"To begin with, we must first change some of the rules.
For starters, you must be totally honest about your surprise.
In return, I'll help you overcome your imminent demise."

Wendy and I looked into each other's eyes.
Could Rumpelstiltskin be trusted with our part of the corporate
   pie?
Could Rumpelstiltskin be trusted, or was his fairy tale legend just a
   big lie?

Wendy and I didn't know what to say.
After all, our boss was out of the office for the day.

About then, up popped a message on my computer screen.

It said, "Win Instantly?—I Don't Think So!!!" in bold 3-D.

"Don't be confused by the computer screen with no logic," Rumpelstiltskin boldly stated.

"My motives are good and honest, you will see.

And my morals are impeccable; if you like, you can go online and see.

But most important of all, you can trust me.

"So let's continue in our quest to solve your problem," Rumpelstiltskin stated with a smile.

"Now listen closely, my rules are quite simple indeed.

We need to act quickly if we are to succeed.

If done properly, the outcome will be positive, you'll soon see.

So leave your concerns and worries at the door, and just follow me."

What to do, what to do, we thought we two.

Could we trust the little man, whom we didn't know?

Could we trust the little man, with a fairy tale past?

Could we trust the little man, who dropped in without being asked?

"Well, well, well" he clapped with much glee.

"There is nothing to fear, I can assure thee.

My intentions are good, this Saturday afternoon.

My intentions are to wipe sadness away from this small, dark room.

My intentions are to spin straw into gold, you'll soon see."

About then he pulled out some fruit from a funny-looking cup.

"Do you see this fruit I hold in my hand, you two?" said he.

"Yes we do," we replied.

In his right hand was an apple, an orange, and a pear.

In the other was a cluster of figs, too big for his hand to bear.

"As you can see, the apple, orange, and pear are soft, mushy, and old.
The figs in my other hand are fresh, sweet, and so nice to hold.

"You see, the dilemma you have is in my right hand. Yes indeed.
You have the same problem as the apple, orange, and the pear tree.
The trees that bore this fruit are old and brittle to the touch.
Now the little fruit they bear just isn't enough.

"You need to escape this pain and imminent death.
You need to attach something that is pleasant in its place, if you hope to find any rest.
You need to attach something that gives you pride in this place.
But remember, you need to attach something that can be hidden from everyone else's face.

"Now watch closely," as he jumped up on the desk.
"I will show you some magic I just learned.
For starters, I'll balance a few things on my magic Robin Hood hat, and then I will add the rest "

Upon his hat he perched a large book.
The title read "Accounting Principles for Beginners" in big black letters as I took a quick look.
And then he spun it round and round as fast as he could.
To our amazement, we watched our book spin.
The book looked as if it were spinning on top of a pin!

We watched in awe, how could this be so.
A book that spins so fast, can it be so.
But to our surprise, he appeared to be in total control.

He raised his hand, demanding attention toward his next quest.

He held up the apple in jest.

He spun it as fast as he could, before putting it in its place.

And there it moved slowly, in its own elliptical space.

Next came the orange.

He quickly prepared it for something great.

Then he carefully moved it into place.

And to our surprise, it too spun into its orbit with equal grace.

The pear was next in line to be spun into place.

But the pear held a special problem, due to the slime on its face.

So he grasped it very carefully, very carefully just in case.

He grasped it with both hands and with much care and grace.

For he knew he must keep from damaging it, if he were to succeed.

For he knew the pear was a special case indeed.

But with much haste, he started to move it into its own special place.

But before I could say, Wow!

Down fell the apple, the orange, the pear, and the book to the ground.

To our surprise, this didn't seem to diminish the finale of his act one bit.

So without hesitation, Rumpelstiltskin took a bow and then picked up his magic stick.

Rumpelstiltskin said, "Now that I've shown you a few of my tricks,

I think you're ready for my next act that I hold in my bag of special tricks.

As we all know, your place here is not very steady.

And quick work will be required if we are to be ready.

"I know this is a time of great stress to each of you.

In a few days, this problem will subside, I can assure you.

In the meantime, we have little time to spare.

Hiding the appearance of the corporate bleed will require some extra care."

Rumpelstiltskin scooted quickly toward our desks, with his magic stick in hand.

Rumpelstiltskin found much paper, including some corporate checks.

In addition, he found notes and questions we had written by hand.

But most important of all, he found numerous opportunities to hide the corporate condition.

As Wendy and I sat down, not knowing what to do.

All we could think was— —is this the right thing to do?

What if we get caught, it's not a pleasant thing to think.

What if we get caught, could we get thrown into the clink?

But all was not black that gray afternoon.

There was also light mixed amongst that potential gloom.

Magic was something we had all watched on TV.

Could Rumpelstiltskin serve up some magic here this afternoon?

We set aside our fears for a while as we thought.

Hopefully our fears would not turn to tears as we mulled our options about.

The fruits of his labor will soon be ours.

The fruits of his labor will soon be a dilemma we just can't toss out.

If we are to halt Rumpelstiltskin's hurried pace.

We must act now, for in an hour it may be too late!

What should we do?

What should we do, we two?

Our thinking processes proceeded with much haste.

We must decide soon, for there is little time to waste.

But then we turned our thoughts to the little man with a feather in his Robin Hood hat.

Was he really our friend, or was this just another fairy tale at that?

Was this something that was simply too good to be true?

We needed to make a decision quickly—we two.

On Monday Morning

On that following Monday morn,

Wendy and I came to work, somewhat forlorn.

It was left over from our previous Saturday paces.

There was just too much to keep from our expressive faces.

Bernie walked into our office and said, "Did you read the front page of the financial news?

Did you read how the press compared me to a modern day Rumpelstiltskin?

You know, a person that can spin glass into gold!"

Then Bernie continued his persistent ranting.

"So tell me, do you have the good news that I have already spread?

Do you have the numbers that will give me the extra money I told everyone I would spend?

Tell me quickly," as he pounded his foot on the floor.

"Tell me the good news, I so much want and more."

Once again, Wendy and I looked into each other's faces.

Once again, we were reminded of our corporate places.

After all, we knew the true meaning of Rumpelstiltskin.

It wasn't about spinning glass into gold, as Bernie would like us to believe.

It was all about uncovering fool's gold, which would require hiding the corporate bleed.

Should we tell Bernie what happened that previous Saturday afternoon?

Or should we let Bernie get angry, hoping he'd stomp right out the door.

And then wishing he would fall right through the floor.

At least that's how the beautiful queen was able to rid herself of Rumpelstiltskin.

⚬ Discovery Notes ⚬

Early in my career, I (Myron) remember a similar situation. It was something akin to, "Let's start from zero and put a man on the moon within the next two weeks." While I'm a proponent of "anything is possible", this demand from a senior manager was too far fetched for even me to comprehend. In this situation, the senior manager demanded that the result appear according to his vision. Looks of bewilderment immediately overtook my team members as they strained to understand the message.

Interestingly, this experience pertained to some financial statistics. I could see the wheels turning in the heads of my coworkers. How could we massage the numbers to get closer to the executive's goal? And guess what happened? It didn't work. Try as we might, we just couldn't get closer to the desired answer without causing other, more severe disruptions in our reporting.

Once this was evident, we stopped trying to "cook the books" or "spin the story" to give the perception that the outcome was achieved. As a team, we stood tall. We bit the bullet and proceeded to inform the senior manager his expectations were unrealistic—before it was too late.

I was proud of each member of the team that day. We stood tall, and we did what was right. We faced the lion, and our greatest fears head on. From that point forward, doing what was right came easy to us.

People the world over generally want to do what is right and to be successful. They also want to be a part of a winning team, and meet their boss's expectations. To do this, they must understand the rules of the road and code of conduct they are expected to follow. These rules and code of ethics must be consistently applied across the corporate landscape without deviation. The continuance of your organization depends on it.

Chapter Ten

The ABCs
of a Strong
Organization

*A story about leadership,
organization, and team building*

Conductors of great symphony orchestras do not play every musical instrument; yet through leadership, the ultimate production is an expressive and unified combination of tones.

Thomas D. Bailey

One of the first elements of a formal education is reciting and singing the ABCs. It is the basis from which most learning evolved. It seems appropriate that a story about the ABCs could serve as a basic foundation for business leadership and organization, similar to that of conducting an orchestra.

This is the story of the alphabet team. A high-powered team that grew to become one, and what they did to sustain their momentum over time. This is a story of leadership and organization, about chemistry and philosophy, and about making the most of the resources available to them. Notice that it all begins with a leader's vision, values, and attitudes toward their internal (Inside) organization, so that they can perform externally (Out) in the marketplace.

R eporter: Thank you for seeing me today. For my first question, I would like to discuss your organizational structure. As you know, there are 26 letters in the alphabet. Was there any special rhyme or reason as to why they were configured in such a manner?"

A: Yes, actually there was a lot of thought and science that went into this project. First and most important, we started with the letter A. If you look at A, you will notice its shape is very simple, yet eloquent. But more important, A's primary shape is a triangle, one of the strongest geometric shapes known to man. And if you look at it from a distance, A is the same shape as a pyramid, a symbol revered since early Egyptian times. We felt it was important that a symbol of strength and energy become the leader of the alphabet team. The letter A captured all the intrinsic elements we were searching for.

Reporter: Wow! I never thought of the letter A in those terms before. Are there other symbols in the alphabet that I might be unaware of?

A: Yes, I believe there are a couple other examples you might find interesting. For example, the letters C, I, and O play the role of building blocks for almost all the other letters—P which contains the letters I and a lower case, inverted C. We refer to C as our comptroller, the letter that keeps our financial books in order. I is our manager of information and O is in charge of operations. As you look through the alphabet, you will see how critical these three letters are in the total composition of our team. This is the group that keeps our team financially strong, informed and productive.

Reporter: Very interesting. Then let me ask you another question about your organization. Were the letters W, X, Y, and Z placed at the end of the alphabet for a reason?

A: A very good question indeed. Yes, we strategically placed these letters at the end of our organizational structure. They are very important. However, we don't want them to be heavily influenced by the senior management team, operations, or marketing and sales. Let me detail the responsibilities of each of these letters and their importance.

First, we refer to W as our "Weight-Lifting Team." They focus on turning over every rock and boulder they can find, in search of market and business intelligence. As you look at the letter W, you will notice it is the largest and widest letter of the alphabet team. Since W is the widest letter, it symbolizes that this unit must scan a broad network of associates on a regular basis and put together intelligence for the management team. We realized early on that remaining distant to the overall operations of the alphabet team would enhance W's value. By being toward the end of the alphabet, they have independence and autonomy, yet still remain committed to the needs of the team.

Do you see what I mean?

Reporter: Yes, I do. Please continue.

A: The next letter is X, or what we refer to as "X Marks the Spot." Here we nurture and launch new products and technologies. You'll notice how X has a center point with tentacles reaching in each direction. Deploying a new product or technology is difficult. The elements important to this unit are identifying potential opportunities on numerous fronts, testing their assumptions quickly, and then moving onto the next opportunity if the previous one failed to materialize. If we identify a winner, we've hit a bull's-eye, which is the center of the letter X. A rapid-fire business process is atypical to the rest of our organization, and therefore X operates as an autonomous unit.

The letter Y refers to "Code Yellow"—our security team. As products, people, and information move throughout our network, everything is monitored by Code Yellow. If something looks suspicious, they attach a red flag to it. If it looks okay, they give it the green light to proceed. Their responsibility is to protect our physical, human, and intellectual resources across our vast network from internal or external intrusion. Therefore, being toward the end of the alphabet is a perfect place for them.

Lastly, the letter Z refers to our "Zorro Team." This is where we use the resources of consultants and outside contractors.

Although they technically aren't a part of our organization, we believe they are an important component of our success. Therefore, we have given them a permanent place on the alphabet team.

I would like to reemphasize one important point about W, X, Y, and Z. There are specific components of our team that we want very close ties with and others that operate more effectively at a distance. The W, X, Y, and Z group is critical to our success; it's just that they operate more effectively from a distance.

Does all this make sense?

Reporter: Yes, indeed. Now that you have explained this to me, I can begin to understand how important organizational structure is to the alphabet team, and how it could pertain to any business.

I see that the letter M is the thirteenth letter, which places it in the middle of the alphabet. Was it placed there for any special reason?

A: Yes, there is a special reason. The letter M is possibly one of the most important letters of the team. It is placed in the middle of our organization, because M is our moral compass. If you look closely, M has two halves. It's as if each half is a beacon that sheds light across the total organization. It is my opinion that any organization lacking a strong moral compass is an organization that will eventually falter. By placing M in the middle of our organization, it becomes difficult to stray from our stated value system.

Reporter: If you don't mind, I would like to move on to another subject.

A: Please do.

Reporter: I understand the phrase, "Choco Choco Chip Chip" is shouted out by various members of the alphabet team from time to time. Where does it come from and what does it mean?

A: The phrase "Choco Choco Chip Chip" evolved from a conversation with T, which oversees our training and team building programs. One day T suggested that we hold a chocolate chip cookie competition amongst the alphabet team. The idea was to have someone from each team make chocolate chip cookies in the company kitchen once a week. They would select the style of cookie (chocolate chunk, chocolate-chocolate chip, etc.), the day of the week, and the time of the day. Then every six months (26 weeks), we would hold a recognition ceremony for categories like Best Chocolate Chip Cookie and Most Improved Chocolate Chip Maker. T went further to explain how the smell of fresh cookies in the oven would be perfect for creating conversation amongst team members. And this activity would activate all of the senses: smell, sight, hearing, touch, and, of course, taste.

When T approached me with the suggestion, I asked if I could think about the idea over a long weekend.

As I thought about the suggestion, I was initially mildly receptive. But over time, my thoughts unfolded into excitement and illumination. What I started to envision was something more than just chocolate chip cookies. Whether we're discussing chocolate chip cookies or an organization, much more happens than many may see. If we go to a store, we see chocolate chip cookies. But it really starts with simple items like flour, sugar, milk, baking soda, and chocolate chips. By themselves, they're unique, yet may not be very exciting. But value begins to unfold when the ingredients are being measured, then added to a bowl, and then mixed. At this point, you have engaged the essential components of the mix. But even at this point, something is missing.

Reporter: Well, of course—you must place the dough in an oven to bake.

A: Exactly! You must put it in an oven to bake. What you're really implying is that for a cookie to reach its peak performance, you must give it adequate time under controlled conditions to develop and unfold. If done properly, something magical occurs. If you undercook or overcook them, the outcome will not meet your desired goals. If the heat is too low or too intense, again the desired outcome will not be achieved.

When you envision an organization like the alphabet team, the same laws of logic and physics must be heeded. You can put the best people into a bowl, but unless you can blend them and then encourage them to grow and engage, the desired outcome is never achieved. Put them under too little heat and the team will not be strong enough to weather the conditions demanded in the marketplace. Put them under too much heat and they will crumble from burnout. Yes, the spirit and strength of the organization can run very deep if done properly. Yet it can be extremely fragile if achieved through shortcuts and lack of guidance.

Reporter: Yes, I see what you mean.

A: When I met with T several days later, I was very excited about my personal revelation regarding their idea. The first thing I said was, "T, do you really know what you have here?"

T stated it would be a good team-building exercise.

I revealed my thoughts to T, and how important their idea was to the total organization. But then I went one step further. I encouraged them to carry their idea to a higher and more meaningful level. From this, several programs emerged. For one, the term "Choco Choco Chip Chip" emerged, and became the rallying cry for the alphabet team. In one situation it might infer a job well done. In another situation it might mean Watch out! Danger ahead (very similar to yelling out "Fore!" on a golf course). It is a saying that has become ingrained in the culture and style of the alphabet team. And since it is unique to us, it carries with it a special meaning— you are part of the team.

We have also built the chocolate chip story into our initiation program for new members. But most important of all, this program became the glue amongst our team members. Through the weekly exercise of making chocolate chip cookies, the team is reminded of the importance of their role to the organization and their relevance to the success of the total team.

Personally, I've been amazed how this simple idea has delivered such positive results. I guess you could say "Never judge an idea by its simplicity."

Reporter: Yes, I see what you mean—there is definitely a magical quality to your story and the saying "Choco Choco Chip Chip."

A: Yes. It's amazing how important the little elements become when building an organization.

Reporter: This is my last question before I go. Businesses generally build their organizations over time. With success, companies will also experience varying degrees of pain and failure. What have you done to get through the tough times?

A: Let me answer your question by telling you a little story about a conversation I once had with a famous business leader.

I asked him, "What's the secret of your success?"

His replied, "Two words."

So I asked him, "What are they?"

"Good decisions."

So I asked a second question, "But how do you make good decisions?"

He replied, "One word."

"And what is that?"

"Experience."

Then I asked him, "And how do you get experience?"

Again he replied, "Two words."

"And what are they?"

"Poor decisions."

Throughout the years of building the alphabet team, we've made some poor decisions. When this occurs, we may be disappointed but not dejected. Because after each failure, we ask ourselves, "What did we learn?" If we can figure out how to harness a few poor decisions, we're confident we'll be better prepared to make good decisions. Due to experience, we know our next attempt will likely succeed.

I must point out one additional aspect of our success. As the leader of the alphabet team, my experience has taught me the importance of feeling the same pain as the rest of the team. It helps when I'm there emotionally with them. Everyone benefits, because the team reenergizes more quickly.

Reporter: Thank you for sharing your secrets with me. I can see the alphabet team will have an enduring place in our culture.

A: And thank you for your interest in the alphabet team. I'd like to leave you with one final message. If the alphabet team is to endure the test of time, the organization must be strong inside, if it is expected to perform on the outside—in the marketplace. In a vibrant organization, there is always strength. And that strength is derived from more than a mere collection of individuals. Enduring strength unfolds when one carefully measures, combines, blends, and then bakes for peak performance.

Yes, strength occurs from the "Inside Out."

Choco! Choco! Chip! Chip!

❧ Discovery Notes ❧

As seen in the story, all members of the ABC organization were valued for their area of specialty and for their personal contributions. So how are these individual efforts blended into powerful teams?

We believe that for a team to truly exist, four prerequisites must be present:

- **Common Vision**—All team members must share the same vision and desire the same end results. They must know where they are going and why it is important for them to get there.

- **Common Mission**—All team members must understand their overall assignment and their individual roles and responsibilities to fulfill their mission. They must know the plan and work the plan.

- **Common Fate**—The team must recognize that they succeed or fail as a unit. Rewards and consequence should be shared appropriately across the entire team.

- **Common Experience**—The people on the team must go through something meaningful together. This can either be a work-related project or an informal team-building session. The goal of this common experience is to build trust, respect, and appreciation for all team members because these values will be tested during the team's work together.

Perhaps the best way to illustrate a highly effective team in action is to observe nature, and the lessons it teaches by example.

Have you ever noticed a flock of geese as they fly? We can learn some valuable lessons about teamwork by watching them fly in formation.[8]

Observation: As a goose flaps its wings, it creates an uplift for the bird immediately behind it. By flying in a V formation, the whole flock adds 71 percent more flying range than if each bird flew alone.

Lesson: People who share a common direction and sense of community can get where they are going more quickly and easily, because they are traveling on the thrust of one another.

Observation: Whenever a goose falls out of formation, it suddenly feels the drag and resistance of trying to fly alone. It quickly gets back into formation to take advantage of the lifting power of the birds immediately in front.

Lesson: If we have as much sense as a goose, we will join teams with people who are headed where we want to go.

Observation: When the lead goose gets tired, it rotates back into the formation and another goose flies at the point position.

Lesson: It pays to take turns doing the hard tasks and sharing leadership. With people as with geese, interdependence with one another is a key to success.

Observation: The geese honk from behind to encourage those up front to keep up their speed.

Lesson: We need to make sure our honking from behind is encouraging, not something less helpful.

---

[8] Adapted from *Agricultural Notes*, Issue 97

Observation: When a goose gets sick, wounded, or is shot down, two geese drop out of the formation and follow their fellow member down to lend help and protection. They stay with the injured goose until it is able to fly again or dies. Only then do they launch out on their own, or with another formation, to catch up with their own flock.

Lesson: If we have as much sense as geese, we'll stand by one another just as they do.

Epilogue
Come
Monday
Morning

Reaching for the next step

The proverbial sweet spot is the magical elixir that many seek. But amid the fervor for revolutionary change, we cannot forget that people are the backbone of a vibrant society... a strong corporation. That morals are the intellectual underpinnings that give people meaning, direction and purpose. That leadership is not about command and control, but rather is about empowerment and being.

These are the intellectual philosophies that deliver results.

t's Monday morning, and you just finished reading this book. As you get ready for work, you reflect on the stories and messages in it. Then your youngest son comes up to you and asks for his weekly school allowance. As you hand over a $10 bill, you find an instant connection to the story about the Three Little Pigs—how your son is similar to Tom Pig. Yes, you know exactly how that money will be spent. It is so predictable. Then your daughter comes down the steps, conservatively dressed like always. Yes, striking similarities to "Consistent-Is-My-Name." Everything has its place, don't expect me to change, and I like everything just the way it is. Then your oldest son, the star quarterback on the high school football team, runs down the stairs yelling, "Get me this and get me that—I'm in a hurry!" Hmmm, a little more "we" and a lot less "me" would be a great improvement for this one. Then you look at your spouse sitting at the kitchen table, reading the morning newspaper and eating breakfast. Yes, definitely the A in the family organization. And lastly, you look at yourself in the mirror. You silently ask yourself, "I wonder which character my family members would identify me as? I'd like to think I'm Little

Red Riding Hood, but might they view me as one of the three Billy Goats Gruff?"

Then you head to work, and you begin to think about your team members, this time in a different light. No longer are their names just Bill, Jim, Susan, and Rebecca. Your team is similar to the chocolate chip cookie dough in the ABC story of "Choco Choco Chip Chip." You were all expected to work together, but you hadn't yet gelled and evolved as a team. This created tension between team members and fostered a poor working environment. Would your members ever resolve their internal issues and evolve as a team?

When you arrive at work, you grab a cup of coffee on the way to your office. As you sit back in your chair, you begin to reflect on the many opportunities, distractions, and challenges that lie just outside your door. Could you become the leader that your group desperately needs? Could you initiate a change environment that keeps everyone onboard, focused, and actively engaged? Could you effectively work with the management team and other departments to develop new, long-term solutions?

S	M	T	W	T	F	S
				1	2	3
4	5	6	7	8	9	10
11	12	13	14	15	16	17
18	19	20	21	22	23	24
25	26	27	28	29	30	31

As you finish your first cup of coffee, you realize the questions you are pondering are not a dream. This is reality. And if you move forward, you recognize that failure is a possibility. Then you remember what the Master Billy Goat said to the three Billy Goats Gruff.

> You must find your youth, if you fear the past.
> You must resist fear itself, if you fear the present.
> You must not fear death, if you are fearful of dying.
> You must not fear love, if what your breathe is the source of life.
> You must challenge your beliefs, if they make you fearful.
> You must become aware, if you hope to find enlightenment.
> You must not fear failure, if you seek success.
> You must not fear what lies over the river, if you love the mountains.

Then you remembered the parting words between Kish and Callie in "The Leadership Safari."

> Callie turned to Kish and said, "Kish, which path should we pursue?"
> Kish responded, "Callie, which path do you want to pursue? It's up to you."

You turn inward and reflect on your situation one more time. "Yes, I am still holding the keys. Yes, the opportunity is mine to seize. Yes, my brilliance lies in my differences—my uniqueness—for that is where my seeds of greatness have been planted."

But then you check your emerging enthusiasm with a degree of doubt. "Can I really make a difference? After all, others have failed before me. And my team members—they don't want more facts and information. They're already overloaded with it. Somehow, they must have faith in me. They must believe that I have the foresight and vision to move mountains. But how?"

As you begin to script out the endless possibilities, you envision Martin Luther King's great speech where he proclaims, "I have a dream..." In your mind, you remember how masterfully the speech was delivered, how emotionally attached people became to his vision, and how it moved a nation.

Then you envision your boss, and how he would have delivered the same message. He would have said something like, "I have a plan, and here are the six things you need to do." Would it be emotionally moving? No! It would have been received with suspicion and doubt. Instead, the Reverend King had a dream! His followers "felt" that story in their heart and soul. And from it, the Civil Rights movement started to move mountains. For millions, it was the foundation for changing the face of interpersonal relationships in America. Yes, his story became history!

If I am to be successful, it's not what I say that will be important, it's what my team members "feel" that will determine my success. If they feel my vision, I believe we can overcome any obstacle. If my vision becomes their vision, we can achieve any goal. However, if they feel that this is the same old song and dance routine they've heard before, my chance for success is minimal.

"Yes, if I am to succeed, I must envision and then deliver a story that gives our struggle meaning. Maybe then our team can evolve and unfold with purpose, direction, and a vision.

"Yes, the path I decide to pursue is up to me."

❧ Discovery Notes ❧

As we test-marketed this book, we noticed that a personal attachment to individual stories would occur. It was random and unpredictable at first. But upon further evaluation, it was evident that people would identify strongly with stories that were relevant in their current lives.

These stories were achieving unexpected relevance in the mind of the reader—a state that can facilitate understanding and change.

Then the next shoe fell. One person with a social services background took a personal liking to several stories. She had worked in California and conducted health clinics where drug addicts and prostitutes would hang out. She noted that the county health agency had reams of information to hand out, but the field employees generally considered the handouts as ineffective. How could you teach when the audience showed little interest in what you had to offer? The old theory goes, You can lead a horse to water, but you can't make it drink. She reasoned that building a teaching curriculum around children's stories could break that proverbial barrier. It's nonthreatening and you can reach people at a level that they can comprehend.

Then we started to test our book in the business world. One day Myron read the story "When Opportunity Knocks—Will You be Ready?" to a corporate client. It was immediately evident that individuals were connecting to specific elements of the story. Jim, Bill, and Ann each felt that they had been passed over for promotion in recent years—they developed an attachment to Rudolph. If called upon, would they be ready for the task? Philip, Jean, and Clara were already part of the elite team. In their minds, they were mulling around the thought that an outsider could become their leader. How would they feel? Could they accept an outsider after being at the top? Then there was Ellen, the CEO. She identified with Santa Claus. She was questioning whether her team was prepared for the rough and turbulent times that lay ahead—the fog bank had already formed in her office. Changes would be needed.

These market research opportunities proved valuable. They tested our assumptions, and we found out that the assumptions were true. To move mountains, leaders must emotionally connect with their employees—employees need to connect with their customers—all because customers want to connect with the products they purchase. But how?

The road to success is already paved, it's just not commonly traveled. That's because we tend to focus on talking to a person's rational brain while we neglect their emotional brain. When we neglect the emotional side of the brain, we tend to be hesitant, a Doubting Thomas of sorts.

The easiest means to reaching the emotional side of the brain is to tell a story.

> *People don't want more information. They are up to their eyeballs in information. They want faith   faith in you, your goals, your success, in the story you tell. It is faith that moves mountains, not facts. Facts do not give birth to faith. Faith needs a story to sustain it—a meaningful story that inspires belief in you and renews hope that your ideas do indeed offer what you promise. Genuine influence goes deeper than getting people to do what you want them to do. It means people pick up where you left off because they believe...*
>
> *A story is your path to creating faith. Telling a meaningful story means inspiring your listeners... to reach the same conclusions you have reached and decide for themselves to believe what you say and do what you want them to do. People value their own conclusions more highly than yours. They will only have faith in a story that has become real for them personally. Once people make your story their story, you have tapped into the powerful force of faith.*[9]

Storytelling can be very powerful. Here is an example of a vision statement from a nineteenth century shipbuilder.

We build Good Ships.
Cheap as we Can,

---

[9] Excerpts from Annette Simmons, *The Story factor; Inspiration, Influence, and Persuasion Through Storytelling.*

Fast if we Must,
But Always Good Ships!

And here's another example from Annette Simmon's book, The Story Factor.

> *A man came upon a construction site where three people were working. He asked the first, "What are you doing?" The man answered, "I am laying bricks." He asked the second, "What are you doing?" The man answered, "I am building a wall." He walked up to the third person who was humming a tune as he worked and asked, "What are you doing?" The man stood up, smiled, and proudly stated, "I am building a cathedral.*[9]

Whether you're always building good ships or building a cathedral, these examples illustrate the power of a good story and how a vision can become your vision.

The stories in *Inside Out* can engage your imagination, just as Dr. King did many years ago. Our stories can help you reestablish the importance of storytelling in your personal, family, and professional life. They can launch your quest for finding your ethnic heritage, teach you the importance of first principles, and provide meaning when clutter and frustration litter your landscape. They can help solidify your vision, provide clarity to your being, and purpose to your goals. And maybe most important of all, storytelling can engage your imagination, so you can daydream your way to success.

Yes, there is hope.

Now it's your turn to use our stories to fit your needs, your vision, your dreams, and your purpose. The baton has been handed to you. Now you must envision and create the energy necessary to move your personal life and/or organization forward in a positive direction.

Now is the time to take that important first step. Take it now!

Author
Contact and Web Page Addresses

We would enjoy receiving your comments and feedback on the information contained in this book, and especially any successes you experienced as a result of the lessons you learned.

Myron's e-mail address is *mradio@the-r-group.com*. Myron's web site is *www.the-r-group.com*.

Rod's e-mail address is *rod@girogroup.com*. Rod's web site is www.girogroup.com.

About
the
Authors

Rod N. Johnson is president of the Giro Group, a consulting firm based in Minnesota. His firm focuses on thought leadership issues relating to change management, strategic thinking, and storytelling in corporate environment. In addition to his work as an executive coach and consultant, Rod writes a monthly newsletter called the "Giro Briefing." Rod has written extensively in numerous trade publications and is a sought-after public speaker.

Rod lives with wife Karen and their son, Justin.

Myron J. Radio is president of The R Group; a consulting firm whose primary focus is to build high-powered teams and develop the people who lead them. Myron offers a complete range of organizational development programs that include meeting facilitation, training, workshops, keynotes and coaching in the areas of change management, strategic and tactical planning, and organizational effectiveness. He is also the author of Dream Makers, a soon to be published allegory for personal development and growth.

Myron lives in the Washington, D.C. area with wife Jeanie and their son, Matt.

Quantity Discounts

Inside Out is available at special discounts for bulk purchases in the U.S. and Canada by corporations, institutions and other organizations. For more information, contact Midwest Bookhouse on the Internet at *www.midwestbookhouse.com* or via phone at 877-430-0044.

Receive the Inside Out *Briefing Free!*

In the global community, knowledge is your competitive advantage. Knowledge that prepares you and your organization on the *Inside!* So you can address the market and the competition on the *Outside!*

The *Inside Out Briefing* is a free online newsletter that provides compelling insights, research, and stories in the areas of personal and professional growth. Each issue includes valuable tips and information about the world in which we live. We encourage you to sign-up today at *www.inside-out-partners.com*. For more information, contact Myron via e-mail at *mradio@the-r-group.com* or Rod at *rod@girogroup.com*.

Remember, if you are to survive and thrive—you must bring clarity, focus and engagement to your goals and your organization.